MW00379692

THE FRONTIER RIFLEMAN

His Arms, Clothing, and Equipment During the Era of the American Revolution, 1760–1800

BY

Richard B. La Crosse, Jr.

ILLUSTRATED BY
Marianne Shepard – Joel Mussman
and

Richard B. La Crosse, Jr.

PIONEER PRESS

Union City, Tennessee

Copyright Pioneer Press, Union City, Tennessee, 1989

All rights reserved. No part of this book may be reproduced in any form without prior written permission from the publisher, except by a reviewer who may quote brief passages in a review to be printed in a magazine or newspaper.

ISBN: 0-913150-57-6

First Printing, August 1989
Second Printing, August 1991
Third Printing, January 1997

Cover painting "American Rifleman" by David Wright ©1985

DEDICATION

To the members of
Schoharie's recreated riflemen,
the intrepid rangers of
Captain Jacob Hager's Company,
15th Regiment of Albany County (New York).

ACKNOWLEDGMENTS

Without the generous cooperation and able assistance of H. Kels Swan, whose museum of Revolutionary War artifacts at Washington Crossing State Park, New Jersey, might well rank as the unsurpassed study collection in existence; the author's blood brother and fellow rifleman, Jim (Jubal) Earley; Erwin Tschanz and his aid in making patterns; and Sharon Cunningham, editor of MUZZLE BLASTS (former editor of Pioneer Press), for faith and patience, this book would not have been possible.

Special attention must go to David Wright, Sherry Schmidt, Ernest Tschanz, Ted Kistner, Allen Burton, Julie Tschanz, Janet Spillane, Mary Ellen Cooper, Glen Jackson, Warren Moser, Gil Dabkowski, Shirley G. McQuillis, William R. Gordon, Lee Hanson and to dozens of historians, curators, librarians and guides who graciously opened up their collections to me at a hundred museums, forts, parks and historical societies from Canada to South Carolina.

TABLE OF CONTENTS

THE RIFLEMAN'S ACCOUTREMENTS

INTRODUCTION

The purpose of this book is to correct preconceived ideas about the American Riflemen; to destroy certain stereotypes and myths that the general public has accepted as truth over the last one hundred and fifty years, and present to those who wish to re-enact or interpret the rifleman's role, a compact conglomeration of his clothing, arms and equipment. Also, it can serve as a guide for any who wish to find out about the smallest detail of their equipment based on the few surviving specimens of the period 1760–1790.

Often called frontiersmen, riflemen, backwoodsmen, scouts, woods-runners, over-mountain men, Big Knives, shirt-tail men – they all refer to the same sort of man. Two differences, however, are the terms "long hunter" or "woodsrunner" which denoted the man, who without a wife or family, lived for periods of time west of the Alleghanys, hunting and trapping and only returning to civilization to trade for a few necessities. Most woodsmen however, would be categorized as frontier farmers, living on the border of the settlements.

Many still believe the myth that the War for Independence was fought by Americans from behind trees, cutting the Redcoats to pieces. Although this was the usual method of fighting on the frontiers, only a few battles of the Revolutionary War were fought in this manner.

The Continental Army was trained in the same manner as European armies of the day and eventually learned to fight successfully that way. The war had to be fought in this manner, at least in the east, because the majority of the men were armed with muskets. The exception were the riflemen who did not fight in lines, but hid behind cover and fired at will, which they could do because of the rifle's greater range and accuracy. There were almost always riflemen in every action of the war.

There is evidence that many riflemen were eventually changed over to musketmen and became regular or line soldiers. But, riflemen who composed only five to ten percent of all the regular troops were an important and essential part of the army.

Though it can be said that the rifle was not the sole reason for the final victory, neither can it be denied that it was the arm that won the early frontier, it being used so successfully against the British and their Indian allies.

When men were sent out to the frontiers to recruit riflemen as the first soldiers of the American Army, they did not have to tell them about liberty or freedom or any such things. They already had their freedom and with their unerring rifles, they kept it . . .

THE FRONTIER RIFLEMAN

"...in the event of Great Britain attempting to force unjust laws upon us by the strength of arms, our cause we leave to Heaven and our rifles."

Hanover Association,
Lancaster County, Penna., 1774

CHAPTER 1

THE RIFLEMAN'S ARMS

The Rifleman's Arms

Much has been written and debated about the rifles effectiveness in attempts to either glorify or debunk it. Perhaps there is room for a few more words on the well-worn subject. When one compares smoothbores to rifles several advantages and disadvantages make themselves evident.

The rifle was accurate to about 300 or more yards, (as opposed to 50 or 60 years for muskets) required about half the powder and two thirds the lead of a musket.

Disadvantage of the rifle was that it took longer to load (about 30 seconds as opposed to a musket which required about 15 seconds), although if the patch was discarded it could be loaded as fast but at the cost of some of its accuracy. Also it could foul up after 10 or 20 shots (depending on the arm itself) and could not normally be fitted with a bayonnet. But it should be brought up that there is little use to firing a smoothbore musket four times a minute and hitting nothing when a rifle could be fired about twice a minute and hit anything larger than five or six inches up to 200 yards every time. Much has been made over its lack of bayonet, but where is there a bayonet with a range of 300 yards?

Admittedly, the rifle was not perfect but it was the best firearm in the world at the time. Eventually the rifle made all other arms obsolete and the woodsman's tactics would become the usual mode of fighting for the world's armies.

But to say the rifle did not win the War for Independence is not to say it could not have if there had been a higher proportion of riflemen. There were several thousand Kentucky and Tennessee riflemen in the War of 1812 who fought with distinction, notably at the Battle of New Orleans in 1815. Also, it should be noted that it was the main arm of the Texans in their war for Independence in 1835-1836 when an "army" of ragtag frontiersmen, armed with rifles defeated a better supplied, well trained Mexican army equipped primarily with muskets and bayonets and who also out numbered them five to one. This is ahead f our story, but it should show the superiority of the rifle. American officers did their best to weed out rifles in the American Army and replace them with muskets, evidently due in large part to military conservatism and the belief that to outfight the British we had to match them at their own game. Military drill and linear tactics were indeed necessary because of the larger numbers of muskets and because of their great inaccuracy, but it seems remarkable that the military could see no additional advantages to the rifle and then tried to capitalize on the advantages of both types of arms.

Nonetheless, the legend of the rifle would become folklore everywhere—by Morgan's Riflemen going through Maine in 1775, by Coffees' Riflemen in Florida in 1814, by Lewis and Clarks' men in the northwest in 1804 and by Jedediah Smith and his trappers in California in 1826—the four corners of the nation.

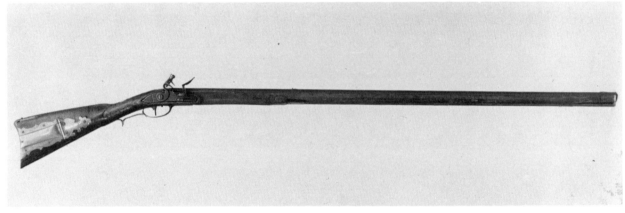

Maker: J. Metzger   **Caliber:** .43
Period: 18th Century   **Barrel Length:** 45¼" (swamped)
Remarks: Barrel is signed in script "J. Metzger" with the raised carved stock of plain
            maple.
Source: Private Collection

Lancaster County Rifle by J. Metzger

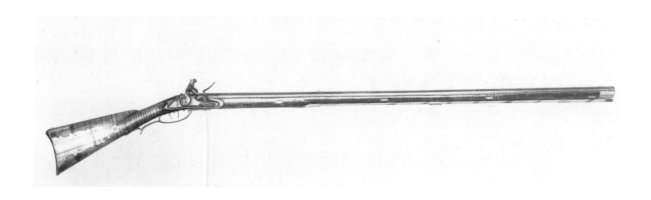

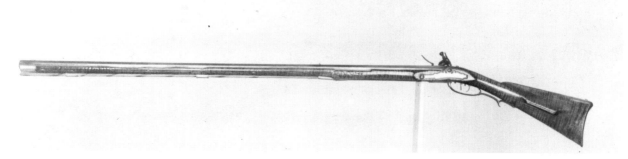

Maker: Jacob Dickert
Period: 18th Century

Barrel Length: 47"
Caliber: .52
Overall Length: 62"

Remarks: Rifle is signed "J/Dickert" on the barrel.
Source: Private Collection

18

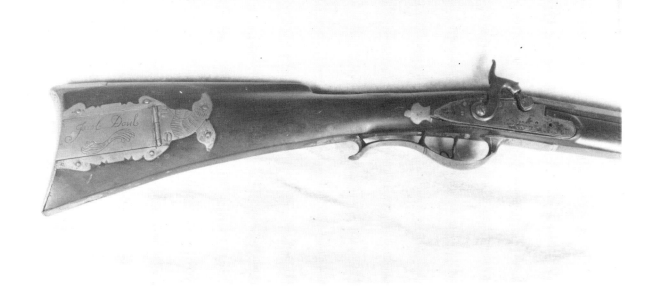

Maker: Jacob Doub
Period: 1790-1815
Overall Length: 49¼"
Barrel Length: 33¼"
Caliber: .49
Flats: 29/32"
Butt Thickness: 1¾"
Source: Allen Burton Collection
Remarks: An early piece, unfortunately changed to percussion. Evidently the barrel was cut down.

Photos by Gilbert Dabkowski

19

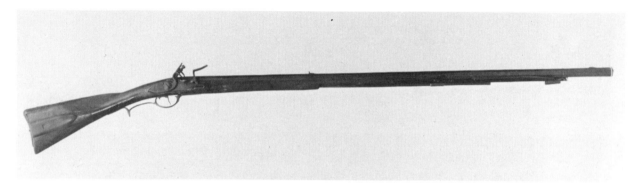

Maker: Unknown   **Caliber:** .43

Period: 18th Century   **Barrel Length:** 43⅛" (Swamped)

Remarks: Stock is maple with a charcoal blued barrel. Rifle is unmarked except for the initials "IHSH" engraved on the buttplate. Rifle is more than likely of Southern origin.

Source: Howard Kendall Collection

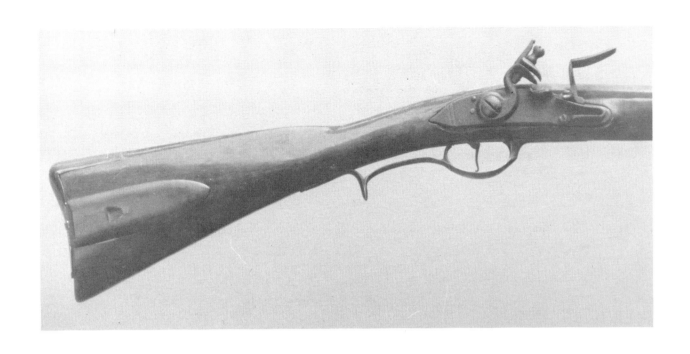

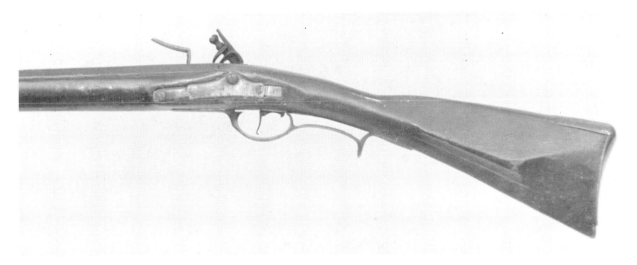

Unknown

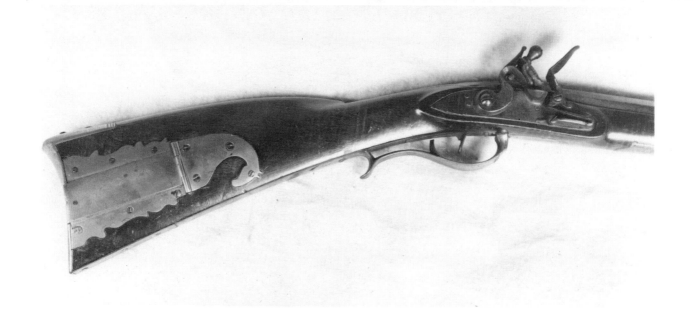

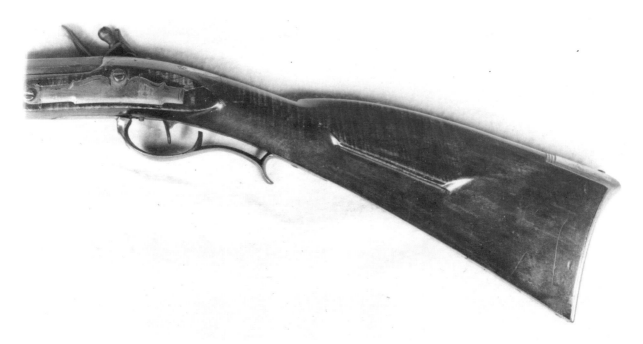

Maker: Unknown

Period: 1760-1800

Overall Length: 54⅛"

Barrel Length: 38¹⁄₁₆"

Caliber: .58

Flats: ⅞"

Butt Thickness: 1¾"

Source: Allen Burton Collection

Remarks: Family tradition states that this rifle served on Benedict Arnold's ill-fated march to Quebec in 1775, but styles indicate a later period of use circa 1795-1830.

Photos by Gilbert Dabkowski

PERIOD PISTOLS – RIFLED HANDGUNS
OF THE 18th CENTURY

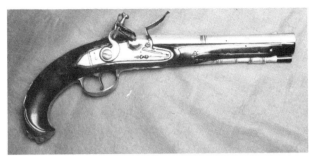 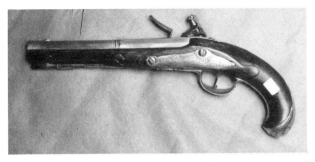

1. From Oley Valley, Pennsylvania, this beautiful specimen has a polished steel barrel and lock. The nosecap is made of horn.
Source: H. Kels Swan Collection. Photos by Gilbert Dabkowski.

 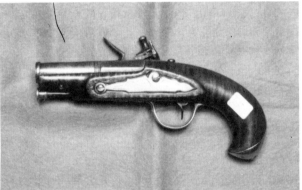

2. Small pocket pistol made by Anthony Dorbach of Cocalico Township, Lancaster County, Pennsylvania.
Source: H. Kels Swan Collection. Photos by Gilbert Dabkowski.

3. A well-made piece with an octagon to round barrel.
Source: Allen Burton Collection. Photographs by Amy Sue Morin.

Maker: Unknown
Period: 18th Century
Overall Length: 13¾"
Source: Private Collection

Barrel Length: 8½" (octagonal to round)
Caliber: .58

CHAPTER 2

MAP AND CHRONOLOGICAL LISTING OF REVOLUTIONARY WAR PERIOD ACTIONS IN WHICH RIFLEMEN WERE INVOLVED, 1774–1782

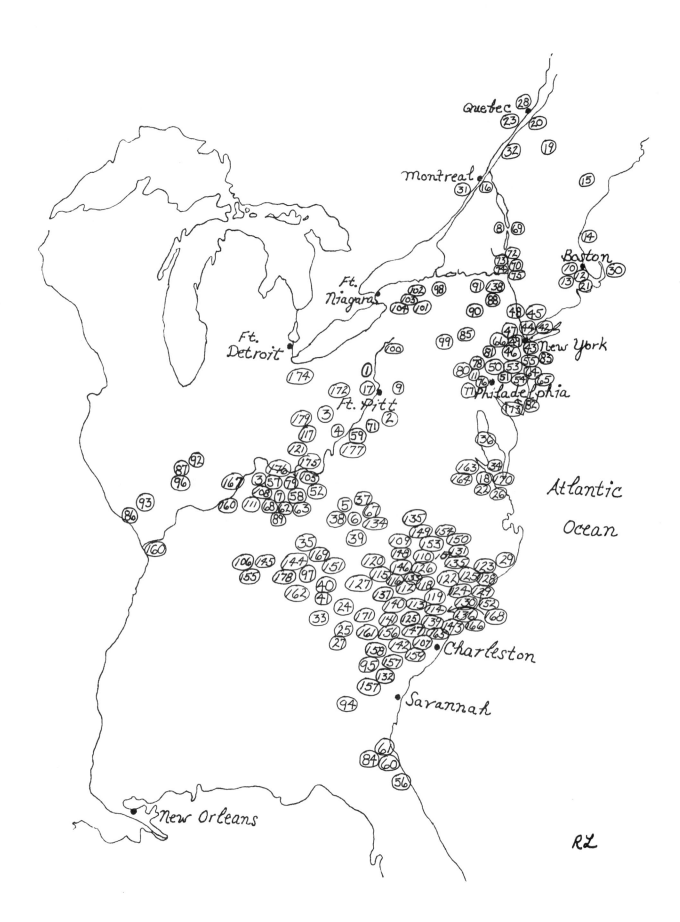

MAP AND CHRONOLOGICAL LISTING OF REVOLUTIONARY WAR PERIOD ACTIONS IN WHICH RIFLEMEN WERE INVOLVED, 1774–1782

This list of battles and skirmishes on the eastern seaboard as well as the western frontier is not complete, nor pretends to be. There were hundreds of actions all along the frontier which accounted for thousands of lives. Presented here are most of the more important such actions.

Also, most of the border fighting in New York State is omitted, as many of those settlers were armed with muskets. However, units not normally thought of as riflemen, such as Vermont's Green Mountain Boys, Marion's Brigade and other partisan forces, are included as they were, at least to some degree, composed of backwoods riflemen.

1774

1. **April 27 – FRONTIER RAIDS**
In early 1774, Indians in the region around Fort Pitt attack settlers in Pennsylvania. Captain Michael Cresap's party kills one Indian and captures another.

2. **April 30 – BAKER'S CABIN MASSACRE, VIRGINIA (now West Virginia)**
Frontiersman Daniel Greathouse and several others, murder six innocent Indians. Logan, the great half-breed Shawnee chieftain, who lost a brother and a sister in the massacre, retaliates and takes thirteen white scalps. The Shawnee go to war!

3. **Summer – HARRODSBURG, KENTUCKY ESTABLISHED**

   August – INDIAN TOWNS SACKED IN OHIO
Major Angus McDonald raids Shawnee towns on the Muskingum River.

4. **October 10 – BATTLE OF POINT PLEASANT, VIRGINIA (now West Virginia)**
Colonel Andrew Lewis leads a column of over 1,000 backwoodsmen down the Kanawha River. Before Lewis can join with another force of almost 1,200 under Lord Dunmore, he is attacked by Chief Cornstalk with 1,000 Shawnee, Miami, Wyandot (Huron) and Ottawas. In the bloody engagement which follows, the Indians are defeated.
> American losses: 200 killed and wounded
> Indian losses: perhaps half
Chief Cornstalk of the Shawnee meets with Dunmore to end hostilities. This results in the opening of the "Dark and Bloody" ground of Kentucky for settlement.

1775

5. **March 10 – THE WILDERNESS ROAD**
From Fort Watauga, Tennessee to the mouth of the Kentucky River, Daniel Boone and thirty axemen blade and cleared a path, via Cumberland Gap. This is in defiance of the Quebec Act, which was enacted by Parliament in 1774, and extended the Province of Quebec to the Ohio River on the south, and to the Mississippi River on the west. By doing so, the British ignored the claims on that western land by Massachusetts, Connecticut and Virginia.

6. **March 17 – SYCAMORE SHOALS, TENNESSEE**
Richard Henderson of the Transylvania Company signs a treaty with the Cherokees and further opens the west to settlement.

7. **April 1 – BOONESBOROUGH, KENTUCKY**
Boonesborough is established at the mouth of the Kentucky River, the second settlement in the area, Harrodsburg having been founded in 1774.

8. **May 10 – FORT TICONDEROGA, NEW YORK**
Ethan Allen and a wild gang of eighty-three backwoods Green Mountain Boys capture Fort Ticonderoga, the first offensive action of the American Revolution.

Ethan Allen – The capture of Fort Ticonderoga.

9. **May 16 – HANNASTOWN, PENNSYLVANIA**
A defense association is formed and a resolution drafted declaring it the duty of Americans to resist English oppression.

June 14 – BIRTH OF THE UNITED STATES ARMY - PHILADELPHIA, PENNSYLVANIA
Congress authorizes the raising of six companies of expert riflemen in Pennsylvania, two in Maryland and two in Virginia.

June 15 – PHILADELPHIA, PENNSYLVANIA
George Washington is elected unanimously by Congress, as Commander-in-Chief of the Continental Army.

June 25 –
Pennsylvania Rifle Battalion is organized. Enthusiasm for the patriotic cause is so overwhelming that instead of the six companies originally called for, nine are raised on the frontier.

10. **July 25 – CAMBRIDGE, MASSACHUSETTS**
The first Continental unit, Captain Doudel's Company of the Pennsylvania Rifle Battalion, arrives in Cambridge.

11. **August 4 – LANCASTER, PENNSYLVANIA**
Captain Michael Cresap's Company, enroute to Cambridge, stop in Lancaster, where they strip to the waist, paint themselves and stage an Indian war dance around a fire in Court House Square.

12. **August 8 – CAMBRIDGE, MASSACHUSETTS**
Captain Daniel Morgan's better disciplined rangers arrive and contrast sharply with other rifle units like Cresap's. Morgan's ninety-six men made the 650 mile march from Virginia in twenty-one days.

Recruiting backwoodsmen for rifle units.

Summer –

Riflemen stage great feats of marksmanship before the amazed New Englanders. They also find time to snipe at the British and kill or wound around sixty, a high percentage being officers. They also fight among themselves, quarrel with the New Englanders, and fire their weapons needlessly.

13. September 10 – **PROSPECT HILL, CAMBRIDGE, MASSACHUSETTS**
    Poorly disciplined riflemen, in protest to the confining of several drunken sergeants, mutiny on Prospect Hill where they are put down by General Washington and 500 troops (including other riflemen). Thirty-three men are convicted of disobedience and mutinous behavior, several are court-martialed, and fines of twenty shillings each are levied. The rifle troops are punished in the worst way – they are no longer exempt from sentry and fatigue duties.

14. September 11 – **ARNOLD'S EXPEDITION TO QUEBEC**
    The rifle captains choose straws, the winners being Captains Hendricks, Smith and Morgan,
    to lead Benedict Arnold's expedition of 1,100 men. At Newburyport, New Hampshire, the troops board eleven schooners to the Maine coast. Indications are some riflemen become seasick.

15. September 24 – **FORT WESTERN, MAINE**
    Benedict Arnold's troops, the riflemen well in advance, move out from
    Fort Western on the Kennebec River, in bateaus.

16. September 25 – **MONTREAL, CANADA**
    Ethan Allen rashly attacks the British and is captured with forty men.

17. September 26 – October 19 – **PEACE CONFERENCE**
    Peace negotiations with Indians at Fort Pitt delay outbreak of border war.

Benedict Arnold
*(After an etching
by H.B. Hall)*

18. **October 24-25 – HAMPTON ROADS, VIRGINIA**
British landing attempt is repulsed and two vessels forced aground are captured by patriot riflemen.

19. **October 25 – ARNOLD'S EXPEDITION IN MAINE**
Four contingents turn back because of difficult terrain and lack of provisions. On one occasion, the riflemen may have, by feigning exhaustion, allowed the New England troops to pass them by, thereby stealing their supply of flour.

20. **November 9 – POINT LEVIS, CANADA**
Arnold's bedraggled force, after suffering untold hardships, reaches the St. Lawrence River at Point Levis.

21. **November 9 – PHIPP'S FARM (OR TECHNER POINT), MASSACHUSETTS**
Nine companies of British light infantry and 100 grenadiers land to seize cattle needed for the Boston garrison. Thompson's Battalion counter-attacks, and after plunging through two feet of icy water, advance on the British forcing them to retreat.
   American losses: two wounded.
   British losses: seventeen killed and two wounded (evidently American Riflemen were aiming for kills).

November 13 – POINT LEVIS, CANADA

22. **November 14 – KEMP'S LANDING, VIRGINIA.**
Americans under Colonel Woodford are dispersed when they attempt to cross a bridge guarded by Lord Dunmore and 350 men. Dunmore then pursues and defeats 150 militiamen who have marched to join Woodford's force.

23. **November 15 – QUEBEC, CANADA**
Benedict Arnold occupies the Plains of Abraham. With 700 men he unsuccessfully tries to bluff the Quebec garrison into surrender.

24. **November 19-20 – FORT "96," SOUTH CAROLINA**
Major Andrew Williamson's 600 Patriots indecisively engage 1800 Tories in a backwoods action.

25. **November 22 – CANE BREAK, SOUTH CAROLINA**
Patriots break up a force of Tories assembling at Reedy River, or Cane Break.

December 8-31 – SIEGE OF QUEBEC, CANADA

26. **December 9 – GREAT BRIDGE, VIRGINIA**
Colonel Woodford defeats Tories and British under Lord Dunmore in less than half hour of surprise action.
   American losses: one man slightly wounded in the hand.
   British losses: sixty-two killed and wounded.
John Marshall, who will later become the first Justice of the Supreme Court, is a lieutenant of the Culpeper Minuteman in this battle. After the Patriots occupy Norfolk, Virginia, Lord Dunmore takes refuge on a ship in the harbor. By January 1, seeing that he cannot retake the town, Dunmore sets fire to Norfolk. It burns for three days, added to by shells from the ship *Liverpool*, to which Dunmore fled in December. Every house in the town is destroyed.

27. **December 22 – GREAT CANE BREAK, SOUTH CAROLINA**
Lieutenant Colonel William Thompson (not of Thompson's Battalion) defeats Tories under William Cunningham.

28. **December 31 – ASSAULT ON QUEBEC!**
In the midst of a blizzard, 800 Americans attack Carlton's 1,800-man garrison. In this desperate gamble, the Americans are repulsed with eighty killed and wounded, and 426 captured. Besides the loss of American General Montgomery, Arnold is wounded, Captain Hendricks is killed and Daniel Morgan is captured. Most of the three rifle companies are also taken.

General Richard Montgomery
(After the painting by C.W. Peale in the Philadelphia Museum)

Winter – BOSTON, MASSACHUSETTS
A brawl occurs between several hundred riflemen and Marbleheads (fisherman-soldiers from Gloucester and Marblehead, Massachusetts under the command of Colonel John Glover), during the siege of Boston. Broken up by an alert General George Washington.

1776

January 1 –
Thompson's Rifle Battalion becomes the first Continental Line under Colonel Edward Hand.

29. February 27 – BATTLE OF MOORE'S CREEK BRIDGE, NORTH CAROLINA
Eleven hundred North Carolina militiamen defeat 1,800 Scottish Loyalists under Brigadier General McDonald in a three minute fight. Numerous rifles on both sides. Fifteen hundred rifles and three hundred muskets are captured by the victorious Patriots.

30. March 7 – HOWE EVACUATES BOSTON
Colonel Edward Hand's riflemen are sent to the New York City area. Three companies of riflemen, sent out to reconnoiter on Long Island, capture a boat, a British midshipman and nine crew members.

31. May 16 – THE CEDARS, CANADA
During the American withdrawal from Canada, 500 Patriots are surrounded and captured by British troops.

May 25 – PHILADELPHIA, PENNSYLVANIA
Congress resolves to commission Indians for military service.

32. **June 8 – BATTLE OF TROIS RIVIERES**
In a three day running fight, 2,000 Americans are dispersed by 6,000–8,000 British troops under General Sir Guy Carleton. Colonel William Thompson is captured, but only one company of riflemen (not Thompson's) are present.

General Sir Guy
Carleton *(From
an engraving by
A.H. Ritchie)*

33. **June 26 – CHEROKEE INDIAN TOWN, SOUTH CAROLINA**
Captain James McCall and his South Carolina Rangers engage Indians. McCall is captured.

July –
Cherokees begin their depredations upon the settlements from southwestern Virginia to northwestern Georgia.

34. **July 8-10 – GWYN'S ISLAND, CHESAPEAKE BAY**
Rebels capture Lord Dunmore's camp and disperse his fleet and forces. Dunmore flees Virginia, but with his latest exploit, brings the colony into the Revolution, firing her citizens with a desire for vengeance that has not previously existed.

35. **July 15 – RAYBORN CREEK (LYNDLEY'S FORT) TENNESSEE**
One hundred fifty Americans under John Downs defeat 200 Indians and Tories in a skirmish. Thirteen American casualties.

36. **July 16 – ST. GEORGE'S ISLAND, MARYLAND**
In his attempt to seize St. George's Island, Lord Dunmore is driven off and withdraws to New York City.

37. **July 20 – ISLAND FLATS, TENNESSEE**
One hundred seventy backwoodsmen sally forth from Eaton's Station and defeat Chief Dragging Canoe (Cherokee) and a like number of warriors.
    Indian losses: at least thirteen killed; unknown wounded.
    American losses: four wounded.
From mid-July to mid-August, eighteen men, two women and several children are killed and two or three captured. Meanwhile, twenty-six Indian scalps are taken.

38. **July 20 – FORT WATAUGA, TENNESSEE**
Seventy-five riflemen under James Robertson and John Sevier are besieged irregularly by 300 Cherokee under Old Abraham for two weeks, until relieved by settlers from Fincastle (Virginia), under Colonel Russell.

39. **July 29 – NORTH CAROLINA INVADES TERRITORY OF THE CHEROKEES**
General Griffith Rutherford, with 2,400 men, begins an invasion into hostile Indian territory and destroys thirty-two towns and villages. The Cherokee power is temporarily broken.

40. **August 1 – ESSENECCA TOWN, SOUTH CAROLINA**
Major Andrew Williamson leads Americans against Indians.
    Indian losses: ninety-four killed and wounded. Seventy-five scalps taken.
South Carolina posts a reward of seventy-five pounds for Indian scalps, one hundred pounds for Indian prisoners and eighty pounds for a Tory or Negro prisoner.

41. **August 8 – ONOCORE, SOUTH CAROLINA**
Major Williamson engages Indians in inconclusive action.
    American losses: five killed and thirteen wounded.

42. **August 25-26 – SKIRMISH ON LONG ISLAND, NEW YORK**
Hand's Pennsylvanians skirmish with Hessians. This brings about a complaint from the Germans concerning such unorthodox methods of fighting.

43. **August 27 – BATTLE OF LONG ISLAND, NEW YORK**
In one of the most mismanaged American defeats of the war, the riflemen suffer heavily. Hand's riflemen, at

Gowanus Road, around midnight or early hours of August 27, are withdrawn and relieved after four days of picket and patrol duty. When Colonel Samuel Miles' 400 riflemen spot the British trap, he sends 170 men of his battalion, under Lieutenant Colonel Brodhead, to the Brooklyn defenses. He and the remaining 230 men attack the rear baggage train of the British. Later, trapped inspite of being forewarned, Miles and 159 riflemen, lacking bayonets, are forced to surrender. Kachlein's Berks County Riflemen are also taken, while the remainder of the 10,000 Americans flee before 22,000 British and German troops.

> American losses: over 1,000 killed, wounded and captured.
> British/German losses: about 400 killed, wounded and captured.

On August 28, Washington encourages the riflemen to keep up their fire, about 100 yards in front of the American defenses.

44. September 16 – BATTLE OF HARLEM HEIGHTS, NEW YORK

In a brief stand, American riflemen under Colonel Moses Rawlings are instrumental in putting enemy to flight One rifleman claims six kills in this battle.

> American losses: thirty killed, 100 wounded.
> British losses: about 200 killed, wounded and captured.

45. September 18 – MUTINY OF MILES' PENNSYLVANIANS

At a joint meeting of Colonel Samuel Miles' Pennsylvania State Rifle Regiment and Atlee's Pennsylvania Regiment of Musketry, 200 men pick up their arms and leave for home, arguing that they do not have to serve outside their own state. At least fifty-eight men return, but force has to be used to restrain them, and one man is bayoneted.

46. October – RELEASE OF PRISONERS AT ELIZABETH, NEW JERSEY

Survivors of the riflemen captured at Quebec on December 31, 1775, are paroled (until January 1, 1777), at Elizabeth, New Jersey. Reportedly only twenty-three of Daniel Morgan's original ninety-six riflemen remain.

47. October 12-13 – BATTLE OF THROG'S NECK, NEW YORK

Thirty of Colonel Hand's riflemen successfully hold off 4,000 British troops under General Howe. After the Americans are reinforced by Regular units, Howe decides to find another landing port.

General Sir William Howe
(From an English print)

48. October 28 – BATTLE OF WHITE PLAINS, NEW YORK

Howe wins a tough fight, attempting to dislodge Washington's troops.

49. November 16 – SURRENDER OF FORT WASHINGTON, NEW YORK

Two hundred fifty Virginia and Maryland riflemen and two hundred Bucks County, Pennsylvania militiamen, in conjunction with 2,000 Regulars, strongly defend Fort Washington against German advances under the command of General Howe. Through the treachery of William Demont, Colonel Robert Magaw's adjutant, Lord Percy has complete plans of the works of the Fort, as well as a statement of the armament and number within the garrison. With this foreknowledge, Howe takes the Fort and the full complement of 2,500 men are taken prisoner. Despite the advantage Demont's treason gives the Hessians, they lose 500 men, and angered by the resistance of the Americans and their heavy losses, begin to massacre the prisoners. British officers immediately stop the slaughter. George Washington, on the opposite bank of the Hudson River, unable to reach Fort Washington in time to save the garrison, witnesses its fall and the killing of the Americans by the Hessians. Most of the American prisoners taken in this section are doomed to die in British prison ships.

50. December 25-26 – WASHINGTON CROSSES THE DELAWARE RIVER

After an inglorious retreat across the Jerseys with Cornwallis at his heels, George Washington takes the offensive. Colonel Hand's riflemen lead the vanguard of the main army.

51. December 26 – FIRST BATTLE OF TRENTON, NEW JERSEY

An American force of 2,400, of which six to eight hundred are riflemen, attack and rout the Hessian command at Trenton in which 1,400 are captured.

Cornwallis *(From the portrait by Hoppner)*

52. December 29 – MC CLELLEND'S STATION, KENTUCKY

Chief Pluggy, a Mohawk chief, a bit out of his country, attacks this frontier fort for two days Simon Kenton is one of the defenders. A short time later, the settlers leave for the east.

October – THROG'S NECK, NEW YORK

53. January 2 – SECOND BATTLE OF TRENTON, NEW JERSEY

Colonel Edward Hand's forces manage to twice delay Cornwallis' vastly superior force advancing on Trenton. On one occupation, a group of riflemen feign a surrender, only to shoot down the Hessians who come forward to take them. Estimate of casualties for British are from thirty to one hundred; for the Americans, about twelve. After holding off British-German forces all afternoon, the rifle troops finally withdraw in good order and aid the main American force in repulsing three assaults over the Assunpink Bridge and Creek. This overlooked action prevented Cornwallis from possibly destroying Washington's army and ending the American Revolution, then and there.

Total British losses: 150-500.

54. January 3 – BATTLE OF PRINCETON, NEW JERSEY

Outnumbered three to one, Washington slips out of Trenton on the night of January 2 and surprises two British regiments at Princeton the next day. The riflemen pursue the fleeing British for miles over the Jersey countryside. Americans destroy the bridge over Stony Brook in an attempt to delay Cornwallis.

Riflemen, with the remainder of the army, go into winter quarters at Morristown, New Jersey. Colonel James Smith, after destroying two parties of British and German troops on his way to join the army, brings his regiment of Westmoreland County, Pennsylvania riflemen into the camp, and is rejected by Washington. The General does not "fall in with the scheme of white men 'turning' Indian." He offers Smith "a major's place in a battalion of rifle men already raised," but as Smith "entertained no high opinion of the colonel" that he would serve under, and with him Smith would "have no prospect of getting my old boys again, I thought I would be of more use in the cause we were then struggling to support, to remain with them as a militia office, therefore, I did not accept this offer."

At Fort Ticonderoga, New York, General Anthony Wayne has trouble with Pennsylvania troops (who actually fire on some New England "Yankees"), and a company of his riflemen (of the 4th Pennsylvania), who decide to go home. This mutiny is put down at gun point; the third recorded mutiny of the rifle troops in less than two years.

55. January 20 – SOMERSET COURT HOUSE (MILLSTONE), NEW JERSEY

American forces, including riflemen drive off British foraging party at Millstone.

56. February 9 – FORT MC INTOSH, GEORGIA

Tories raiding from St. Augustine, Florida, force the surrender of Patriots.

March – DANIEL MORGAN'S RIFLE CORPS FORMED

Brigadier-General Daniel Morgan

Colonel Daniel Morgan, back in action from his imprisonment after the failed assault on Quebec in December, 1775, picks 500 riflemen from the army at large and forms them into a well disciplined and well trained, crack unit of rangers. The men, from Pennsylvania, Virginia and Maryland are commanded by Lieutenant Colonel Richard Butler (not to be confused with Tory Colonel John Butler of Butler's Rangers), Major Lewis Morris of New Jersey (killed at Edge Hill, Pennsylvania, December 8, 1777), and the following captains: Cobel, Posey (later Major, and an important rifle commander), Knox, Long (later sent with his company to the Schoharie Valley in New York), Swearingen (captured at Saratoga, New York), Parr (later Major, and another important rifle commander. He and his men are also sent to the Schoharie Valley), Boone (sent home to Northumberland, Pennsylvania after wounds received. He is killed at Fort Freeland, Pennsylvania on July 29, 1779), and Henderson, all able officers.

57. March 18 and 28 – HARRODSBURG, KENTUCKY

Hotly pursued, James Ray warns the settlers when 200 Shawnees under Blackfish, unsuccessfully attack on March 18. The Indians make another visit, also unsuccessful, on the 28th.

58. April 24 – BOONESBOROUGH, KENTUCKY

Between forty to one hundred Shawnee ambush the station's defenders outside the walls. As the riflemen fight their way back to the stockade, young Simon Kenton saves Daniel Boone's life three times.

59. May 2 – GUNPOWDER SHIPMENT
Lieutenant William Linn, one of George Rogers Clark's chief scouts arives at Fort Henry, Virginia, (now West Virginia), with ninety-eight barrels of powder after a remarkable journey from New Orleans.

60. May 15 – SAWPIT BLUFF, FLORIDA
Indians steal forty horses form Colonel John Baker, who tracks the Indians down and steals the horses back.

61. May 17 – THOMAS' SWAMP, FLORIDA
Colonel John Baker and 109 Americans are routed by British rangers and Indians.
   American losses: eight killed; thirty-one captured.
   (Indians murder fifteen of the prisoners).

62. May 23-24 – BOONESBOROUGH, KENTUCKY
Unsuccessful Shawnee attack on this fort.

63. May 30 – LOGAN'S STATION, KENTUCKY
The same band of Shawnee take a swing at Benjamin Logan's station, thirty miles from Boonesborough.

64. June 17 – MILLSTONE, (SOMERSET COURT HOUSE), NEW JERSEY
Morgan's riflemen harass an entrenching British force.

65. June 22 – BRUNSWICK, NEW JERSEY
Morgan, pushing down the right bank of the Raritan River, puts the Hessian picket guard in retreat, and hotly pursues them. Enemy is pushed back to Piscataway in a spirited action. General Anthony Wayne follows, but does not catch up in time to give much aid.

66. June 26 – SHORT HILLS, NEW JERSEY
Captain James Darke, with a detachment of Morgan's Rifle Corps, participates in the action commanded by American General Lord William Alexander Stirling, near Metuchen, New Jersey. Outnumbered ten to one, the Americans retire after a brief stand. Morgan's men pour an accurate fire from the rear and flanks into the British Army all the way to Rahway.

67. July 2 – TREATY AT LONG ISLAND, TENNESSEE
Cherokee Indians, defeated by frontiersmen, cede lands to Virginia and North Carolina.

William Alexander,
General Lord Stirling
*(From the engraving
by G.R. Hall)*

68. July 4 – BOONESBOROUGH, KENTUCKY
Blackfish unsuccessfully attacks Boonesborough for two days.

69. July 7 – BATTLE OF HUBBARDTOWN, VERMONT
In a rear guard action after the American evacuation of Ticonderoga, New York, militia under Colonel Seth Warner are defeated by Hessians and British commanded by Baron Friederich Von Riedesel and General Simon Fraser. The costly delaying action, however, permits the main American force under General Arthur St. Clair to escape pursuit. Enemy officers fall prey to deadly rifle fire in this engagement.

70. August 16 – BATTLE OF BENNINGTON, VERMONT (Actually fought in New York State)
New Hampshire militia under General John Stark and the Green Mountain Boys commanded by Colonel Seth Warner, totally destroy a 1,000 man foraging force of British and Hessians. (The song, "Riflemen of Bennington," was written to commemorate this American victory).

71. September 1 – SIEGE OF FORT HENRY, VIRGINIA (now West Virginia)
Four hundred Indians besiege Fort Henry until Major Samuel McCulloch, pursued by Indians near Fort Henry, rides his horse down a 150 foot cliff to escape across Wheeling Creek and lead reinforcements back to lift the siege. Indians possibly lose sixty to one hundred killed and wounded. (Some writers have mistakenly written that the white renegade, Simon Girty, led this attack, but Girty, an American militiaman at the time, did not turn traitor until 1778).

General John Stark
*(From the painting
by H.B. Hall)*

Riflemen pick off British columns.

72. September 17 – SWORD'S FARM, NEW YORK

Morgan's regiment, sent to the northern army under General Horatio Gates, ambush a British foraging party and kill, wound and capture thirty of the enemy in action very close to the British lines.

73. September 19 – BATTLE OF FREEMAN'S FARM (Saratoga, New York)

Morgan's riflemen, strung out along a fringe of woods, fire a ragged volley on a British advance force, dropping almost all the officers and artillerymen immediately. The British, assisted by German troops, hold the field, but at twice the cost of men of the American forces. The British-German losses are about 600 men, possibly two-thirds of whom fall in front of Morgan's riflemen, supported by General Henry Dearborn's light infantry.

Horatio Gates
(After the portrait by Stuart)

Major-General Henry Dearborn

74. October 7 – BATTLE OF BEMIS HEIGHTS (Second Battle of Saratoga)

Morgan's riflemen again distinguish themselves by smashing British-German resistance. They are ably led by Benedict Arnold. One rifleman, historically noted as Tim Murphy, picks off Sir Francis Clerke and General Simon Fraser at 300 yards, turning the tide of the battle. Many British officers are killed today.

British losses: 600 killed, wounded and captured.
American losses: 400 killed, wounded and captured.

About twenty-three American riflemen are killed or wounded on this campaign.

75. October 17 – SURRENDER OF BURGOYNE, SARATOGA, NEW YORK

Outgunned and outnumbered, Burgoyne surrenders his remaining 5,700 men to General Horatio Gates. After this surrender, Colonel Morgan refuses Gates' offer of involvement in his plot to succeed Washington as Commander-in-Chief.

76. December 6 – CHESTNUT HILL, PENNSYLVANIA

After a return march of eighteen days to rejoin Washington's force in Pennsylvania, Morgan's riflemen, on November 17, attack Germans near Fort Mercer, New Jersey, inflicting twenty to thirty casualties. Only 160 riflemen are reported to have shoes. On December 6, flanking parties of Washington's and Howe's forces skirmish.

77. December 7 – EDGE HILL (WHITEMARSH), PENNSYLVANIA

Howe's Redcoats, sallying forth from Philadelphia, are stopped by Morgan's riflemen an Massachusetts troops who "mess up" the British lines. The riflemen, due to attrition, illness and forced marches and who are only 175 strong, fire upon advancing British, fall back into the woods to reload and keep up a deadly fire, when the enemy charges. Morgan loses twenty-seven killed and wounded, including Major Lewis Morris (killed). Seventeen other Americans are wounded. For the riflemen, it is a heavier loss than at Saratoga.

Burgoyne

78. December 19 – VALLEY FORGE ENCAMPMENT

Morgan leaves the 11th Virginia on furlough and in his absence the rifle corps is commanded by Major Thomas Posey. In this encampment the Continental troops suffer fearfully, losing over 2,000 men to disease, malnutrition and exposure.

The burial of General Fraser.

Washington and Lafayette at Valley Forge
(From the painting by Alonzo Chappell)

79. **February – CAPTURE OF SALT MAKERS, BLUE LICKS, KENTUCKY**
Captain Daniel Boone and thirty riflemen who are boiling salt, are taken captive by over 100 Shawnee warriors near Blue Licks. Boone manages to convince the Indians not to attack the now defenseless Boonesborough.

March 17 – VALLEY FORGE ENCAMPMENT
A brawl is narrowly averted on St. Patrick's Day, when an effigy of St. Patrick is raised in mockery by New England troops camped next to Morgan's 11th Virginia, most of whom are of Irish descent.

80. **May 1 – HATBORO, PENNSYLVANIA**
An American outpost, composed of Pennsylvania militia, is driven off by a vastly superior British force.

81. **May 20 – BARREN HILL, PENNSYLVANIA**
Some of Morgan's riflemen, under Captain James Parr, attempt to "oppose and retard" General Clinton's British troops. However, after exchange of fire, the enemy marches back to Philadelphia. About fifty Oneida Indians take part in this action. General Lafayette, consequently, escapes a trap planned for him.

82. **June 28 – BATTLE OF MONMOUTH, NEW JERSEY**
Following the British retreat across the Jerseys, a force of George Washington's Life Guards and Morgan's riflemen capture fifteen British grenadiers on, or around, June 24, near Allentown, New Jersey. The next day more are picked up at a nearby mill.
   At Monmouth, Morgan receives confusing orders from General Charles Lee and misses the battle.

83. **June 28-30 – BRITISH WITHDRAWAL FROM THE JERSEYS**
Morgan's riflemen stay on British heels all the way to Sandy Hook, New Jersey.

Sir Henry Clinton

Major-General Charles Lee (From the engraving by G.R. Hall)

84. **June 30 – ALLIGATOR BRIDGE, FLORIDA**
American cavalry is repulsed by the Tory East Florida Rangers. Colonel Elijah Clarke, a noted backwoods partisan leader, is wounded.

85. **July 3-4 – WYOMING VALLEY, PENNSYLVANIA "MASSACRE"**
Two hundred twenty-seven Americans are killed and scalped by a force of 900 Loyalists and Indians under Colonel John Butler. Actually, most, if not all, of these settlers are immigrants from Connecticut rather than frontier riflemen.

86. **July 4 – KASKASKIA, ILLINOIS**
From Redstone, Pennsylvania, down the Ohio and across to the Mississippi River, George Rogers Clark's men march and take Kaskaskia without firing a shot.

87. **July 20 – VINCENNES, INDIANA**
Clark's riflemen take another important British post at Vincennes. Clark's position is a very dubious one, being deep in Indian Territory. His intent is to knock out the British posts supplying the Indians.

George Rogers Clark *(From the portrait by Jouett)*

Massacre at Wyoming Valley, Pennsylvania

CLARKS ADVANCE AGAINST VINCENNES.

On they went across the Horse Shoe Plain, four miles of wading in water, sometimes breast high.

88. August – NEW YORK TORIES DISPERSED

Captain Gabriel Long's company of riflemen ambush and disperse a company of Tories under Captain Charles Smith. Captain Long personally kills and scalps Smith, and sends the trophy to General John Stark in Albany. After this affair, Christopher Service, a noted Tory, is dispatched by the legendary Tim Murphy and Dave Ellison.

89. September 7-19 – BOONESBOROUGH, KENTUCKY

About 400 Shawnee under Blackfish, and fifty Canadians and British attempt the capture of Boonesborough for the third time. Negotiations, trickery, assaults with flaming arrows and an attempt to tunnel under the walls of the fort, all fail. Thus, thirty riflemen and some boys successfully hold off a determined force ten times their size. Over 125 pounds of lead are dug out of the stockade walls and re-melted for rebel rifles.

> American losses: two killed, four wounded (Jemina Boone is one of those wounded).
> Indian losses: 37 killed, and many more wounded.

After the siege, Captain Boone is acquitted of charges of treason (for surrendering at Blue Licks), and conspiracy (for his friendly attitude toward his Indian captors), and because of his successful defense of the fort, is, instead of being court martialed, promoted to Major by the settlers.

Colonel Daniel Boone.
(From a portrait by Chester Harding, owned by Colonel R.T. Durrett, Louisville, KY.)

90. October 6 – RAID ON UNADILLA, NEW YORK

Major Posey's riflemen and Colonel William Butler's 4th Pennsylvania destroy Unadilla, Onaquaga, and ten miles of crops along the Susquehanna River in retaliation for a Tory-Indian raid on German Flats, New York in September.

91. November 11 – CHERRY VALLEY MASSACRE

Embittered by the loss of Unadilla, the Iroquois Indians under Joseph Brant and Butler's Rangers massacre soldiers and civilians. Posey's riflemen are called into action, but are not in time to catch the enemy.

92. December 17 – BRITISH RETAKE VINCENNES, INDIANA

Lieutenant Colonel Henry Hamilton with 500 English, French and Indians, take the lightly defended town. Clark, who returned to Kaskaskia after taking Vincennes in July, had left only a handful of his precious few men under the command of a Mr. Helm, to defend the town through the winter. Hamilton, also counting on the lack of military activity during the dead of winter, sends the bulk of his force back to Detroit, keeping only one hundred men with him at Vincennes.

<u>1779</u>

British harassment of locals.

93. February 6 – CLARK ADVANCES ON VINCENNES, INDIANA

Clark leaves Kaskaskia, Illinois, with 150 men (including some French volunteers), to arrive at Vincennes on February 23.

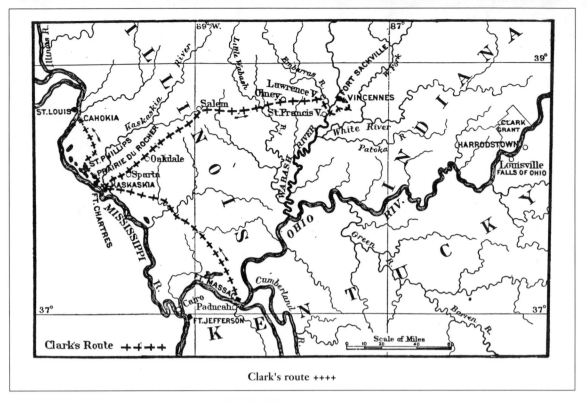

Clark's route ++++

94. February 10 – CAR'S (sic) FORT, GEORGIA
Skirmishing between British and local militia.

95. February 14 – BATTLE OF KETTLE CREEK, GEORGIA
Colonel Andrew Pickens and militia, 300 strong, defeat 700 Tories, mostly Scotsmen, under a Colonel Boyd (killed).
  American losses: nine killed and twenty-three wounded.
  Tory losses: forty killed and seventy-five captured. In addition, five more Tories are hanged.
This affair adds greatly to Patriot spirits.

96. February 23-25 – VINCENNES, INDIANA
After one of the most heroic marches in military history, Clark's riflemen attack Fort Sackville. After murdering five Indians in full view of the horrified garrison, Clark receives the surrender of the post. The commander, Colonel Henry Hamilton, is sent in chains to Williamsburg, Virginia, and held there for the rest of the war. This time, the area comprising the present states of Indiana and Illinois are held by the Americans for all time.

96A. FORT JEFFERSON, KENTUCKY
After the conquest of the Illinois country, Clark establishes a fort overlooking the Mississippi River – America's westernmost fort. (After repelling Indian attacks by the Choctaws and Chickasaws, the fort is abandoned in June, 1781).

97. April – CHICKAMAUGA, TENNESSEE
North Carolina and Virginia troops led by Colonel Evan Shelby (Isaac's father), successfully destroys the towns of the Chickamauga Indians.

98. April 20 – ONONDAGA TOWN, NEW YORK, DESTROYED
Parr's riflemen, under Lieutenant Elijah Evans from the Schoharie Valley, act as scouts and flankers on a highly successful raid on an Iroquois village. A quantity of muskets and rifles are taken on this raid.

99. July 29 – FORT FREELAND, PENNSYLVANIA
Three hundred British troops and Iroquois Indians capture Fort Freeland and a number of settlers. When Captain Hawkins Boone and thirty-two riflemen attempt to relieve the fort, they are attacked and all, except thirteen who make good their escape, are killed during the fight or put to death later, including Captain Boone.
  American losses: one hundred eight killed, wounded and captured.
  British-Indian losses: eight-ten killed; unknown wounded.

100. August 11-September 14 – ALLEGHANY RIVER, PENNSYLVANIA EXPEDITION
Colonel Daniel Brodhead, with 600 men march from Fort Pitt up the Alleghany River and destroy ten Indian villages in northern Pennsylvania.

101. August 29 – BATTLE OF NEWTOWN, NEW YORK (Now Elmira)
To chastise the Iroquois Indians of western New York, Washington sends 5,000 Continental troops under General Sullivan to destroy the Indian towns and to take Fort Niagara. About 110 riflemen, under Captains Long and Simpson, and several militia units act as scouts and flankers for the army. The rifle corps skillfully detects a Tory-Indian ambush on the Chemung River and immediately engages them. This leads to a large scale battle and the total rout of the 1,200 man enemy force, by the remainder of the Americans.

Major-General John Sullivan *(From a family portrait)*

102. September 10 – CANADAIGUA, NEW YORK BURNED
Sullivan's troops burn a large Seneca town of well-built houses, crops and orchards.

103. September 13 – GROVELAND AMBUSCADE
A party of twelve riflemen and fourteen musketmen under Lieutenant Thomas Boyd, are ambushed by 400-500 of John Butler's Rangers and Iroquois Indians and are almost completely wiped out within a few minutes; not, however, before taking a hefty toll of the enemy. Only Tim Murphy, Captain Johokiam (an Oneida scout) and a few other Americans escape.

104. September 14 – DESTRUCTION OF GENESEO, NEW YORK
This is the farthermost point reached by Sullivan's troops, and here the mutilated forms of Lieutenant Thomas Boyd and Sergeant Michael Parker are discovered. Apparently, upon being questioned by Butler, Boyd talked but none the less, was brutally tortured and killed by the Iroquois.

(**Note:** Although this expedition destroyed forty Indian towns and kept the Iroquois off balance for a few months, the Indians, still loose, continued to raid the New York and Pennsylvania frontiers with renewed ferocity. Sullivan had failed in the east with 5,000 troops, in what George Rogers Clark had succeeded at with only 150 backwoodsmen in Indiana and Illinois).

105. October 4 – LICKING RIVER, KENTUCKY
White renegade, traitor and ex-long hunter, Simon Girty and his Shawnee warriors, ambush and destroy frontier riflemen on the Ohio River.
    American losses: fifty-seven killed, wounded or captured. Thirteen escape.

November – END OF CONTINENTAL RIFLEMEN
Riflemen under Major James Parr, now at West Point, New York, have their rifles taken away and are issued muskets. They then return to their previous regiments (in which they were members before being drafted into Morgan's Rifle Corps in 1777). The riflemen under Morgan himself, had disbanded in the Fall of 1778; some whose enlistments have expired, go home, and others are drafted into other regiments.

At this point, there are few, if any, riflemen left in the United States Army.

1780

106. Winter – FORT NASHBOROUGH, TENNESSEE
Colonel James Robertson establishes a settlement, or station, on the Cumberland River in Tennessee. Other stations already established in the area are Ascher's, Armstrong's, Bledsoe's, Barton's, Buchanan's on Old French Lick, Donelson's at Clover Bottom, Eaton's, Freeland's, Fort Union (Haysboro), Kilgore-Mauldin (Cross Plains), and Renfroe's on Red River. Altogether, only 256 riflemen are counted.

107. May 12 – CHARLESTON, SOUTH CAROLINA SURRENDERS
Five thousand American regulars and militia under General Benjamin Lincoln surrender to the British in the worst American defeat of the war. Included is the old 11th Virginia (later the 7th Virginia), now a part of the 1st or 2nd Virginia detachment. It is questionable, however, just how many were really former rifle troops.

108. June 20 – RUDDLE'S STATION, KENTUCKY
Alexander McKee and Captain Henry Bird with a force of 1,200 Indians and British, and a six-pounder cannon, force the surrender of Ruddle's Station, the first fort in Kentucky to fall to the British.

109. June 20 – RAMSOUR'S MILLS, NORTH CAROLINA
Colonel Moore's 700 Tories are routed by Colonel Francis Locke's 400 Patriots. There were probably rifles on both sides.

Major-General Benjamin Lincoln (Painted by J. Herring from the original by Colonel Sargeant in the collection of the Massachusetts Historical Society)

110. June 28 – MARTIN'S STATION, KENTUCKY
Colonel Henry Bird and Alexander McKee with 700 Indians armed with a six-pounder, force the capitulation of Martin's Station, making in all, four stations captured. Bird, afraid of depredations by his Indian allies, orders a withdrawal. Of 350 settlers captured, some 200 become unaccounted for; possibly some became Tories, but many more were tomahawked on the journey to Detroit.

111. July 12 – WILLIAMSON'S PLANTATION, SOUTH CAROLINA
Ninety Patriots defeat 115 Tories in a surprise dawn attack.
  American losses: one killed.
  Tory losses: thirty to forty killed; fifty wounded.

112. July 14 – PACOLETT RIVER, NORTH CAROLINA
Georgia Patriots defeat Tories.

113. July 15-16 – MC DONNELL'S CAMP, SOUTH CAROLINA
Three hundred Tories defeat fifty-two Americans.

114. July 20 – FLAT ROCK, SOUTH CAROLINA
Colonel William R. Davie wins a skirmish against the Tories.

115. July 30 – THICKETY FORT, SOUTH CAROLINA
Colonel Isaac Shelby captures a Tory fort without firing a shot.

116. August 1 – ROCKY MOUNT, SOUTH CAROLINA
General Thomas Sumter is repulsed when his 600-man militia fails to take a Tory outpost.

117. August – CHILLICOTHE AND PIQUA, OHIO
In retaliation for Captain Bird's invasion of Kentucky, George Rogers Clark assembles nearly 1,000 riflemen, and after defeating Shawnee warriors, destroys two great Shawnee towns.

118. August 1 – GREEN SPRINGS, SOUTH CAROLINA
Major James Dunlap, with sixty Tory dragoons and 150 Tory mounted riflemen are repulsed by Colonel Elijah Clarke's 186 men. Casualties, about 15% on both sides.

119. August 6 – HANGING ROCK, SOUTH CAROLINA
Colonel Davie, partisan leader, annihilates three companies of Tories and captures sixty horses and 100 rifles and muskets; then proceeds from Rocky Mount with eighty patriots and defeats 500 Tories.
American losses: twelve killed, forty-one wounded.
British losses: one hundred ninety-two killed and wounded.

120. August 8 – CEDAR SPRINGS, SOUTH CAROLINA
Militia under Elijah Clarke and Isaac Shelby skirmish inconclusively with a Tory force twice their size under Major Patrick Ferguson.

121. August 9 – LITTLE MIAMI RIVER, OHIO
George Rogers Clark defeats a band of Shawnee and destroys another major Indian town.

122. August 13 – FORT CAREY (WATEREE FERRY), SOUTH CAROLINA
Militia under Colonel Thomas Tyler captures British wagon trains (36 wagons) and take thirty prisoners.

123. August 15 – PORT'S FERRY, SOUTH CAROLINA
Francis Marion and 250 partisans rout a party of Tories under Major Micajah Gainey with a loss of two wounded. Tory losses unknown.

124. August 15-16 – GUM SWAMP, SOUTH CAROLINA
A midnight surprise action between Gates' and Cornwallis' armies. Major John Armstrong's North Carolinians act as flankers, along with light infantry, both strung out in Indian file.

125. August 16 – BATTLE OF CAMDEN, SOUTH CAROLINA
In one of the worst American defeats, 1900 Americans are lost. An unknown number of riflemen are present.

126. August 16 – FISHING CREEK, SOUTH CAROLINA
Colonel Banastre Tarleton gains an overwhelming victory over Sumter's partisans, while losing only sixteen men, himself.
American losses: 150 killed, 300 captured and forty-four wagons taken.

127. August 18 – MUSGROVE'S MILLS, SOUTH CAROLINA
Mountain men under Colonels Elijah Clarke and Isaac Shelby repulse Tories, and kill sixty-three, wound ninety and capture seventy men.
American losses: four killed, eight wounded.

128. August 20 – GREAT SAVANNAH (NELSON'S FERRY), SOUTH CAROLINA
Francis Marion surprises and routs British and Loyalist force, kill and capture twenty-four and retake 150 Continental prisoners.
American losses: one killed, one wounded.

129. August 27 – KINGSTREE, SOUTH CAROLINA
Marion and 150 Patriots clash indecisively with 300 British and Tory forces under Major James Wemyss.

130. September 4 – BLUE SAVANNAH, SOUTH CAROLINA
With only fifty men, Marion routs 200 Tory militia under Colonel Jesse Barefield, after the Patriot advance guard overruns a forty-five man advance guard of Tories.

131. September 12 – CANE CREEK, NORTH CAROLINA
Skirmish between local militia and Tory troops under Major Patrick Ferguson.

132. September 14-18 – FORT GRIERSON AND AUGUSTA, GEORGIA
Colonel Elijah Clarke and Lieutenant Colonel James McCall capture two forts, but are repulsed at the Tory stronghold, White House, at Augusta.
Tory losses unknown.
Indian losses: twenty killed, more wounded.
American losses: sixty killed, and wounded, and twenty-eight hanged by Tories.
Colonel Ferguson gives chase to Colonel Clarke.

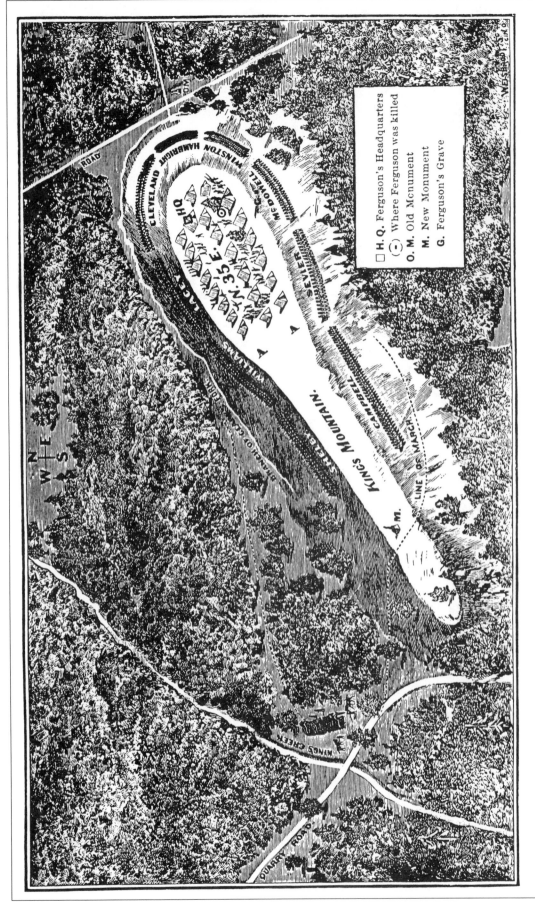

Diagram of the Battle of King's Mountain

133. September 21 – WAHAB'S PLANTATION, NORTH CAROLINA

Colonel William Davie, with seventy mounted riflemen under Colonel William Davidson, and eighty mounted partisans, rout a British force under Major (later Colonel) George Hangar.

American losses: one wounded, accidentally.

British losses: fifteen to twenty killed, forty wounded.

134. September 25 – SYCAMORE SHOALS, TENNESSEE

With nearly all rebellious opposition put down east of the mountains, Colonel Patrick Ferguson decides to cross over and disperse the hated mountain men. One thousand mountaineers who rendezvous on the Watauga River at Sycamore Shoals, decide to head east and attack Ferguson first!

135. September 26 – CHARLOTTE, NORTH CAROLINA

Americans under Colonel William Davie, Colonel William Davidson (with two companies of riflemen, seventy strong) and Major Joseph Graham, engage Cornwallis' advance guard. The first two British assaults are turned back, the third succeeds and the American force is pursued vigorously for several hours.

American losses: twenty killed and wounded.

British losses: fifteen killed and wounded.

136. September 29 – BLACK MINGO CREEK, SOUTH CAROLINA

Francis Marion's partisans are initially rebuffed, but rally and take a strong Tory outpost under Colonel John C. Ball.

American losses: two killed, eight wounded.

Tory losses: three killed, twenty wounded.

137. October 7 – BATTLE OF KING'S MOUNTAIN, SOUTH CAROLINA

Under the able leadership of Colonels William Campbell (with 400 Virginia riflemen), Benjamin Cleveland (with 350 North Carolina riflemen), John Sevier (with 240 over-mountain men) and Isaac Shelby (with another 240 over-mountain men), a total of 1,400 riflemen of the farmer, hunter and Indian fighting class, march to intercept Major Patrick Ferguson and his 1,100 Loyalists (composed of 1,000 musketmen and 100 riflemen). About 950 Patriot riflemen, all mounted on good horses, push ahead to King's Mountain, after camping near the Cowpens. Ferguson and his men, all Tories except their leader, attempt to hold the height with the bayonet, while the backwoodsmen, or "the yelling boys," assail with the rifle. Twice the Tories force the Patriots down the slopes only to have the riflemen find cover or reload on the run, turn about and chase them back up the mountain. The third time this happens, the backwoodsmen swarm up, take the position, kill Ferguson with eight rifle balls and continue killing the surrendering Tories until order is resumed.

American losses: twenty-eight killed, sixty-four wounded.

Tory losses: one hundred fifty-seven killed, one hundred sixty-three wounded, six hundred ninety-eight captured.

The superiority of rifles and bush tactics over muskets and military tactics, at least on the frontier, is proven once more.

138. October 15 – MIDDLE FORT, NEW YORK

Twelve hundred British, Loyalists, Indians and Hessians under Joseph Brant and Sir John Johnson sweep up the Schoharie Valley, burning and pillaging everything in their path. At the Middle Fort, garrisoned by 204 Continental and militia men under Major Melancthon Woolsey, the latter attempts to surrender but is physically prevented from doing so by the rifles of Tim Murphy and Dave Ellison in their greatest moment. Unaware of the drama within the stockade, the enemy force continues up the valley.

139. October 26 – BLACK RIVER, SOUTH CAROLINA

Francis Marion surprises and routs Tories in a night attack.

Tory losses: three killed, fourteen wounded, twenty-three captured, and eighty horses taken.

Some of the captured Tories willfully join Marion's force.

November – OTARI, (OVERHILL CHEROKEES) ONCE AGAIN BEGIN RAIDING ON THE SOUTHERN FRONTIER

140. November 9 – FISHDAM FORD (BROAD RIVER), SOUTH CAROLINA

Two hundred fifty British fail in a night attack on General Thomas Sumter's 550 men.

A few days later, Marion, lacking ammunition fails in an attack on Georgetown, South Carolina.

The Death of Major Patrick Ferguson – King's Mountain

141. November 20 – BLACKSTOCKS (TIGER RIVER), SOUTH CAROLINA
General Sumter's 1,000 men have the better of Colonel Tarleton's 270 Tories in a hard fought engagement. Riflemen were present on the American side under Colonels Hampton, Twiggs and Clarke.
>American losses: three killed, five wounded.
>Tory losses: fifty killed.

142. December 11 – LONG CANE, SOUTH CAROLINA
Colonel Elijah Clarke skirmishes with forces under British Lieutenant Colonel Isaac Allen.

143. December 12-13 – HALFWAY SWAMP, SINGLETON, SOUTH CAROLINA
Inconclusive skirmish between Marion's partisans and British regulars.

General Thomas Sumter (After the portrait by C.W. Peale)

144. December 16 – BOYD CREEK, TENNESSEE
Colonel John Sevier and 100-300 riflemen from the Watauga and Nolichucky River, ambush approximately seventy Cherokee warriors and kill at least thirteen. No American losses. Seven hundred horsemen under Major Joseph Martin and Colonel Arthur Campbell burn 1,000 Indian cabins, and destroy 50,000 bushels of corn. Twenty-nine more warriors are killed and seventeen women and children captured with only one white killed and two wounded.

1781

145. January 15 – FREELAND'S FORT, TENNESSEE
After James Robertson returns from the Kentucky settlements with badly needed salt, the Indians stealthily sneak into the settlement, but are driven out by Robertson's men.
>Indian losses: two killed, two wounded.

146. January 17 – BATTLE OF COWPENS, SOUTH CAROLINA
In one of the most brilliantly fought battles of the war, General Daniel Morgan destroys Colonel Banastre Tarleton's force of 1,100 British and Tories. Morgan's force has 200 Virginia riflemen, 140 others under Davidson, and McDowell's 200 North Carolina and Georgia militia riflemen. Out of a total of 1,040 troops at least 540 are riflemen.
>American losses: twelve killed, sixty wounded.
>Tory losses: one hundred killed (including thirty-nine officers), two hundred twenty-nine wounded and six hundred captured (almost 90% of British-Tory force is taken).

General Morgan now retires from the area, and is unsuccessfully pursued by Lord Cornwallis.

Colonel Banastre Tarleton

147. January 24 – GEORGETOWN, SOUTH CAROLINA
Francis Marion and "Light Horse Harry" Lee harass a Tory stronghold.

148. February 1 – CATAWBA RIVER (COWANS FORD), NORTH CAROLINA
Three hundred North Carolina militiamen, many of them riflemen under General William Davidson, unsuccessfully attempt to contest the British crossing of the river. Davidson is killed in this engagement.

149. February 6 – SHALLOW FORD, NORTH CAROLINA
A skirmish during General Nathanael Greene's race to reach the Dan River ahead of Cornwallis.

150. February 25 – HAW RIVER (PYLE'S DEFEAT), NORTH CAROLINA
"Light Horse Harry" Lee's detachment of cavalry, in pursuit of a plundering expedition under Tarleton, runs into three hundred Loyalist recruits on their way to join Cornwallis. Fearing the loss of his strike at Tarleton, Lee, trusting to the resemblance of uniforms, tries to slip by the Loyalists undetected. He is in the midst of them when one of their riflemen notices the Patriots and fires. The blow at Tarleton now lost, Lee's detachment kills ninety-nine Loyalists in the space of only a few minutes. With their commander, Pyle, wounded, the remainder flee in all directions.

Tarleton at Cowpens, South Carolina

During this race to the Dan River, a detachment of 700 riflemen under Colonel Otho Williams, covers the retreat, harasses and misleads Cornwallis, who is in pursuit of the main body of the American Army, intent on its destruction. Williams attacks in hit-and-run raids at both Clapp's Mill and Wetzel's Mill. At Wetzel's, Patriot riflemen, at very close range, fire and miss British Lieutenant Colonel James Webster in a rare demonstration of poor shooting.

American losses: twenty killed and wounded.

British losses: at least twenty-one killed and wounded.

151. March – CHEROKEE TOWNS DESTROYED IN TENNESSEE
John Sevier and 150 mounted backwoodsmen attack the Cherokees, killing thirty warriors, burning five towns and taking 200 horses. Only one American killed and one wounded.

General Henry Lee –
"Light-Horse Harry"

152. March 6 – WIBOO SWAMP, SOUTH CAROLINA
Tories are routed by Francis Marion and lose several men.

153. March 15 – BATTLE OF GUILFORD COURTHOUSE, NORTH CAROLINA
Lord Cornwallis, with 2,000 troops defeat Greene's 4,300 (part Continental Army, part militia) in a costly American action. Present are at least 400 riflemen under Colonels Charles Lynch and Richard Campbell, who are used on the right and left flanks. At each point where the main army retreats, the riflemen are the last to leave, inflicting heavy losses on the British. Greene's hope to repeat the Cowpens fight fails to materialize. The two corps of riflemen under Lynch and Campbell suffer heavily, having, of their complements, 113 killed, wounded and missing (according to a report by American General Otho Williams).

154. March 21 – BEATTIE'S MILL, SOUTH CAROLINA
Colonels Elijah Clarke and McCall capture a British force with a loss of thirty-four Americans killed or wounded. Major James Dunlap, the British commander, may have been murdered after his capture at this battle.

155. April 2 – FORT NASHBOROUGH, TENNESSEE

At the appearance of a small body of Indians, twenty mounted riflemen give chase and are ambushed, but with the help of their hunting dogs, fight their way back into the stockade.

American losses: five killed, two wounded.

Indians suffered several casualties.

156. April 15-23 – FORT WATSON, SOUTH CAROLINA

Without artillery, Francis Marion and "Light Horse Harry" Lee capture the fort by seizing the post's water supply (by simply placing Captain McCottry's riflemen at the fort's spring out of musket range), and building a "maham tower." This latter was a high tower built of logs enabling the riflemen to enfilade the fort. While the fort is being attacked, the men inside have no way to defend it without exposing themselves to the aim of the sharpshooters.

American losses: two killed, six wounded.

British losses: one hundred-sixteen killed, wounded or captured.

General Francis Marion
(From an engraving by H.B. Hall)

157. April 16-June 5 – SIEGE OF AUGUSTA, GEORGIA

Militia under General Andrew Pickens and Colonel Elijah Clarke and Continentals under "Light Horse Harry" Lee, surround and besiege a post held by Colonel Thomas Brown. On May 23-24, Pickens and Clarke intercept a party of the garrison and falling upon them, kill and capture British soldiers amounting to six companies. Also, mountaineers under Isaac Shelby, help stop and drive back Tories under a Major Dill. A "maham tower" is used with effect by riflemen. Brown surrenders Augusta on June 5.

American losses: forty killed and wounded.

British losses: fifty-two killed, 334 captured.

158. May 11 – ORANGEBURG, SOUTH CAROLINA

Lee and Marion force the surrender of a British/Tory garrison.

159. May 12 – FORT MOTTE, SOUTH CAROLINA

Lee and Marion, by resorting to flaming arrows, force the fort to surrender.

British losses: one hundred-fifty captured.

General Andrew Pickens
(From a copy by John Stolle of the original painting by Thomas Sully, owned by Mr. Clarence Cunningham, Charleston, S.C.

Summer –

Major James Parr raises 300 Continental riflemen in Pennsylvania.

**Major-General
Nathanael Greene**
(From Trumbull's portrait)

160. June – FORT JEFFERSON, KENTUCKY

This fort is abandoned by the Americans as being untenable.

161. June 10-29 – SIEGE OF NINETY-SIX, SOUTH CAROLINA

During the twenty day siege of this post by General Nathanael Greene, a "maham tower" is again built for riflemen and used to great effect. However, when the Americans assault the fort, the Tory commander counter attacks, and finding cover in a defilade, cannot be shot at by the riflemen. This unsuccessful siege costs the Americans one hundred eighty-five killed and wounded.

British losses: twenty-seven killed, fifty-eight wounded.

162. June – STRIKES AGAINST CHEROKEE INDIANS

John Sevier with one hundred mounted riflemen leads a succession of blows against the Cherokee in which twelve Indians are killed and scalped.

LAFAYETTE CALLS ON MORGAN

Marquis de Lafayette, in dire need of rifle troops in his Virginia campaign, calls on General Daniel Morgan in Winchester, Virginia, who responds by leading a body of Shenandoah Valley riflemen to the French commander's aid.

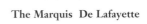

The Marquis De Lafayette

163. June 26 – SPENCER'S TAVERN, VIRGINIA
Simcoe's Rangers and Hessian jaegers are set upon by an American force, including riflemen under Majors Call and Willis, in a sharp conflict. Evidence indicates the riflemen were mounted, although they may have fought on foot in the action.
> American losses: nine killed, fourteen wounded and fourteen missing, (of which numbers the riflemen lost one killed, eight wounded and thirteen missing from the total).
> British losses: at least thirty-three killed and wounded.

Anthony Wayne *(From a sketch by Colonel Trumbull)*

164. July 6 – GREEN SPRING, VIRGINIA
Lord Cornwallis' entire British force of 7,000, lures General Anthony Wayne's 900 Pennsylvanians into ambush. The riflemen, in advance give a good account and manage to extricate themselves. The Continental Regulars boldly attack and lose heavily before retiring.
> American losses: one hundred forty-five killed, wounded and captured.
> British losses: seventy-five killed and wounded.

165. July 17 – QUINBY'S BRIDGE, SOUTH CAROLINA
Through several blunders, General Thomas Sumter fails in an attack on British defenses.

166. August 13 – PARKER'S FERRY, EDISTO RIVER, SOUTH CAROLINA
Francis Marion ambushes and routs 200 British dragoons and claims the enemy lost 100 killed and wounded.

167. August 25 – LOCHRY'S DEFEAT, OHIO RIVER, INDIANA
Joseph Brant, Mohawk Chief, with 100 Tories and Indians surprises and defeats the same number of Pennsylvania militia riflemen, who are coming to reinforce George Rogers Clark, near the Big Miami River.
> American losses: about half captured and half killed, Captain Lochry among the latter.

168. September 8 – EUTAW SPRINGS, SOUTH CAROLINA
British under Colonel Stuart (after the return of Lord Rawdon to England) repulse General Nathanael Greene's troops with heavy casualties on both sides. Riflemen are evidently present in Marion's Brigade and other militia units. The British then retreat to Charleston.

169. September 11 – MOCCASIN CREEK, TENNESSEE
After a family is massacred on Moccasin Creek, John Sevier and 200 mounted riflemen retaliate by striking deep into Indian territory and destroying several Chickamauga and Creek towns on the Coosa River.

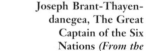

Joseph Brant-Thayen-danegea, The Great Captain of the Six Nations *(From the portrait by G. Romney)*

170. September 29-October 19 – YORKTOWN, VIRGINIA
On September 29, riflemen skirmish with the German Anspach Battalion on the Hampton Road. The siege of Yorktown begins on September 30, and out of 9,000 American Continentals and militia, there are as many as 780 frontier riflemen under Colonel William Campbell, and 100-300 Continental riflemen. However, Lafayette fears some of his riflemen under Campbell, who could stay for as little or as long as they pleased, might go home in time for the harvest; so, it is questionable just how many riflemen may have been left during the siege of Yorktown.

On October 19, Lord Cornwallis surrenders his 8,000 troops in the last major battle of the war on the eastern seaboard.

171. November 27 – FAIR LAWN, SOUTH CAROLINA
Joint command of Colonels Isaac Shelby and Hezekiah Maham, with 200 backwoodsmen and the Carolina Dragoons, take a strong British post.

1782

172. March 7-8 – GNADENHUETTAN MASSACRE, OHIO
Militia led by Colonel David Williamson, invades this village of Delaware Indians (who had been converted

The Battle of Eutaw Springs
(From the painting by Chappell)

The surrender of Cornwallis
(From Trumbull's painting in the Rotunda of the Capitol at Washinton)

to Christianity by Moravian missionaries), and captures 100 men, women and children. Although the Indians offer no resistance, resentment against them for an earlier attack on a white settlement in western Pennsylvania leads to the execution of the Delawares by the frontiersmen.

173. April – RIFLEMEN GO NAVAL
Captain Joshua Barney uses Bucks County sharpshooters in place of marines on his privateer "Hyder Alley" (sixteen 6-pounders) with a total crew of 120. On the Delaware River, Barney meets the "General Monk" (twenty 6-pounders, and formerly the "General Washington"), and retakes her. The riflemen pick off all who attempt to fight on the decks or rigging. The "General Monk" again becomes the "General Washington."

174. June 4-5 – SANDUSKY, OHIO
Colonel William Crawford leads a force of mounted backwoodsmen from Mingo Bottom, Pennsylvania, 150 miles to Sandusky, Ohio, where he is attacked by 100 of Butler's Rangers under Captain William Caldwell, and 200 Indians under Captain Pipe and Wingenund of the Delaware, Zhaus-sho-toh of the Wyandots (Huron), and the white renegades Simon Girty, Alexander McKee and Matthew Elliott. (These last three were frontiersmen who led Indian raids against the encroachment of the westward-moving settlers). After the Tories and Indians are reinforced by Shawnee and other Lake Indians, most of the riflemen succeed in breaking out of the encirclement. Several are captured and horribly tortured, including Colonel Crawford, Major William Harrison and William Crawford (Colonel Crawford's nephew). It was reported by Dr. James Knight, who later escaped, that Girty sat back and enjoyed the spectacle, and that Colonel Crawford died heroically. John Slover, another noted woodsman, also made good his escape.

175. August 15 – BRYAN'S STATION AND BATTLE RUN BRANCH, KENTUCKY
While the major attack by the Indians is to be launched on Bryan's Station, seventy warriors manage to draw out Captain Holder and other mounted riflemen from Hay's, McGee's and Strode's Stations, and ambush them at Battle Run Branch, inflicting some loss on them.

On August 15, Captain William Caldwell, Alexander McKee, Matthew Elliott, Simon and George Girty, with 300 Wyandots and other Indians, attack Bryan's Station. Thinking he can take it by surprise, Simon Girty leads his warriors in an assault on the stockade (a rare occurrence, despite the movies), only to be greeted by a blast of accurate fire from forty rifles. Girty sends part of his men to ambush a relief force, and succeeds only in slowing them down. Girty fails to burn out the settlers, and withdraws on the eventual approach of the relief force.

176. August 19 – BLUE LICKS, KENTUCKY
Proceeding against Daniel Boone's warnings, 182 Kentuckians led by Colonel Todd, McGary and Boone are ambushed by Simon Girty and 400 warriors. Approximately seventy of the frontiersmen are killed (including Israel Boone, Daniel's son), or captured. Indian losses vary from sixteen to sixty-four. This is the last major frontier battle on Kentucky soil.

177. September 11-13 – FORT HENRY, WEST VIRGINIA
Some forty Tories and 250 Indians fail to take the settlement in this attack led by James Girty. (This may be the battle where Elizabeth Zane, only sixteen years old, saves the fort by retrieving badly needed powder).

178. September 20 – LOOKOUT MOUNTAIN, TENNESSEE
John Sevier leads backwoodsmen in victory over Tories and Indians. It is said that all told, Sevier engaged and defeated the Indians in some forty skirmishes and raids.

The fighting in Tennessee was probably the only sector of the long American frontier in which the Indians suffered more losses than the settlers.

179. November 10 – CHILLICOTHE, OHIO
About 1,100 mounted riflemen rendezvous on the Licking River in Kentucky under General George Rogers Clark and moving north, rout the Shawnee at Chillicothe, Ohio, burning several villages in revenge for the mismanaged affair at Blue Licks, Kentucky, in August.
Note: On September 12, 1782, a settler, in a letter to the Governor of Virginia, stated that in six years in the territory claimed by Virginia "eight hundred and sixty fell, the matchless-massacred victims of their [Indians] unprecedented cruelty".

CHAPTER 3

THE TRUE ROLE OF RIFLEMEN IN THE REVOLUTION

THE TRUE ROLE OF RIFLEMEN IN THE REVOLUTION

Authorities and historians have forever debated the importance and achievements of frontier riflemen in the Revolutionary War. It has been an easy matter for those with pro or con opinions to point out those battles which most clearly illustrate their views. Others, intending to be more moderate in their dealings with the subject, seek a balance by simply choosing a few victories and defeats, adding positive and negative contemporary accounts, and letting it go at that.

But what is the actual truth? That the riflemen were the elite, and were instrumental in winning the war; that riflemen were an undisciplined, worthless set of rogues who were more of a liability than a help to the American Army; or, an exact balance of these two extremes? This study would suggest none of these.

No doubt the critical reader could find actions not listed here that would offset these statistics, but I believe the chronology to be an accurate statement of the riflemans' performance. For those actions in which it is believed half or more of the American force was composed of riflemen are based on careful estimates of the troops involved. Partisans like Elijah Clarke, Thomas Sumter and Francis Marion undoubtedly had men armed with rifles but it is impossible to say how many.

Debunkers have been quick to point out the serious lack of discipline of the early rifle units of 1775, conveniently overlooking the fact that there were no more complaints in this regard by 1777. It was a very real problem largely ironed out in less than a year. In the spring of 1776, Washington did not want to lose his "First Regiment of the Continental Line," a unit of Pennsylvania riflemen, and wanted their re-enlistments lengthened as ". . . the loss of such a valuable and brave body of men will be of great injury to the service . . . They are, indeed, a very useful corps . . ." Even the losses sustained by the riflemen at the Battle of Long Island (August 27, 1776) was not quite the "rifle defeat" some would have us believe – their casualties (largely among Miles' Pennsylvania State Rifle Regiment) seem to have been in proportion to the losses of the Continental Army at large. And while, of course, their performance in victorious actions can be seen, some defeats such as the assault on Quebec (December 31, 1775), Fort Washington (November 16, 1776), or Freeman's Farm (September 19, 1777) can serve as examples hardly less than valorous. Interestingly, their most disastrous defeats were at the hands of the Indians and Loyalist Rangers at Blue Licks (August 19, 1782) and Crawford's defeat (June 4-5, 1782).

By and large, the most successful riflemen were the over-mountain men of Tennessee. Under the capable leadership of Isaac Shelby, James Robertson and John Sevier their continual successes in the Cherokee campaigns as well as against the Loyalists and British in the east can hardly be overrated. And, certainly the monumental campaigns of George Rogers Clark and his tiny army of riflemen on the old Northwest frontier are some of the greatest achievements in the military history of the world.

Wars are not fought or gauged like a baseball or football season with wins or losses, but this is a good indication of the overall performance of riflemen during this critical period in America's development.

I believe this to be the first such study of a battle-by-battle analysis of the effectiveness of the riflemen and will let it stand as an eloquent answer to the detractors.

CHAPTER 4

SUMMARY OF ACTIONS OF
FRONTIER RIFLEMEN 1774-1782
WINS, LOSSES, AND INCONCLUSIVE ACTIONS

SUMMARY OF ACTIONS OF FRONTIER RIFLEMEN 1774-1782

(*Denotes actions in which most or all the American troops were riflemen)

WINS	LOSSES	INCONCLUSIVE
1774 Baker's Cabin Massacre (April 30)* Indian Towns Sacked in Ohio (August)* Battle of Point Pleasant, West Virginia (October 10)*	Logan's Retaliation (May)	
1775 Ft. Ticonderoga, New York (May 10) Siege of Boston (1775-76) Hampton Roads, Virginia (October 24-25)* Phipp's Farm (Lechner Point), Massachusetts (November 9)*	Montreal (September 25) Kemp's Landing, Virginia (November 14)	Fort "96," South Carolina (November 19-21)
Cane Break, South Carolina (November 22) Great Bridge, Virginia (December 9)* Great Cane Break, South Carolina (December 22)	Quebec (December 31)	
1776 Moore's Creek Bridge, North Carolina (February 27)* Skirmish on Long Island, New York (March 7)*	Cedars, Canada (May 16) Trois Rivieres, Canada (June 8) Cherokee Indian Town, South Carolina (June 26)*	
Gwyn's Island (Chesapeake Bay) (July 8-10) Rayborn Creek, Tennessee (July 15)* St. George's Island, Maryland (July 16) Island Flats, Tennessee (July 20)* Ft. Watauga, Tennessee (July 20)* North Carolina Invades Cherokees (July 29)* Essenecca Town, South Carolina (August 1)*		

WINS	LOSSES	INCONCLUSIVE
		Onocore, South Carolina (August 8)*
		Skirmish/Long Island, New York (August 25-26)*
	Long Island, New York (August 27)	
Harlem Heights, New York (September 16)*		
Throg's Neck, New York (October 12-13)*		
	White Plains, New York (October 28)	
	Ft. Washington, New York (November 16)	
Trenton, New Jersey (December 26)		
McClelland's Station, Kentucky (December 29)*		

1777

WINS	LOSSES	INCONCLUSIVE
Second Battle of Trenton, New Jersey (January 2)*		
Battle of Princeton, New Jersey (January 3)		
Somerset Court House, New Jersey (January 20)*		
	Ft. McIntosh, Georgia (February 9)	
Harrodsburg, Kentucky (2 attacks March 18 & 28)*		
		Boonesborough, Kentucky (April 24)*
Sawpit Bluff, Florida (May 15)		
	Thomas Swamp, Florida (May 17)	
Boonesborough, Kentucky (May 23-24)*		
Logan's Station, Kentucky (May 30)*		
Millstone, New Jersey (June 17)*		
Brunswick, New Jersey (June 22)*		
	Short Hills, New Jersey (June 26)	
Boonesborough, Kentucky (July 4)*		
	Hubbardton, Vermont (July 7)	
Bennington, Vermont (August 16)		
Ft. Henry, West Virginia (September 1)*		
Sword's Farm, New York (September 17)*		
	Freeman's Farm, New York (September 19)	
Bemis Heights, New York (October 7)		
Chestnut Hill, Pennsylvania (November 17/December 6)		
Edge Hill (Whitemarsh), Pennsylvania (December 7)		

WINS	LOSSES	INCONCLUSIVE
1778		
	Capture of Salt Makers, Blue Licks, Kentucky (February)*	
	Hatboro, Pennsylvania (May 1)	Barren Hill, Pennsylvania (May 20)
British Withdrawal from the Jerseys (June)		
	Alligator Bridge, Florida (June 30)	
	Wyoming Valley, Pennsylvania (July 3-4)	
Kaskaskia, Illinois (July 4)*		
Vincennes, Indiana (July 20)*		
New York Tories Dispersed (August)*		
Boonesborough, Kentucky (September 7-19)*		
Raid on Unadilla, New York (October 6)		
	Vincennes, Indiana (December 17)*	
1779		
		Car's Fort, Georgia (February 10)
Kettle Creek, Georgia (February 14)		
Vincennes, Indiana (February 23-24)*		
Ft. Jefferson, Kentucky (February)*		
Chickamauga, Tennessee (April)*		
Onondaga, New York (April 20)		
	Ft. Freeland, Pennsylvania (July 29)*	
Alleghany River Expedition, Pennsylvania (August-September)		
Battle of Newtown, New York (August 29)		
	Groveland Ambuscade, New York (September 13)*	
	Licking River, Kentucky (October 4)*	
1780		
	Charleston, South Carolina (May 12)	
	Ruddle's Station, Kentucky (June 20)*	
Ramsour's Mills, North Carolina (June 20)		
Williamson's Plantation, South Carolina (July 12)		
	Martin's Station, Kentucky (June 28)*	

WINS	LOSSES	INCONCLUSIVE
Pacolett River, North Carolina (July 14)		
	McDonnell's Camp, South Carolina (July 15-16)	
Flat Rock, South Carolina (July 20)		
Thickety Fort, South Carolina (July 30)*		
	Rocky Mount, South Carolina (August)	
Chillicothe, Piqua, Ohio (August)*		
Green Springs, South Carolina (August 1)		
Hanging Rock, South Carolina (August 6 – two victories)		
		Cedar Springs, South Carolina (August 8)
Ft. Carey, South Carolina (August 15)		
Port's Ferry, South Carolina (August 15)		
		Gum Swamp, South Carolina (August 15-16)
	Camden, South Carolina (August 16)	
	Fishing Creek, South Carolina (August 18)	
Musgrove's Mills, South Carolina (August 18)*		
Great Savannah, South Carolina (August 20)		
		Kingstree, South Carolina (August 27)
Blue Savannah, South Carolina (September 4)		
		Cane Creek, North Carolina (September 12)
Ft. Grierson, Georgia (September 14-18)		
Augusta, Georgia (September 14-18)		
	White House, Georgia (September 14-18)	
Wahab's Plantation, North Carolina (September 21)		
	Charlotte, North Carolina (September 26)	
Black Mingo Creek, South Carolina (September 29)		
King's Mountain, South Carolina (October 7)*		
Middle Fort, New York (October 15)		
Black River, South Carolina (October 26)		
Fishdam Ford, South Carolina (November 9)		
Blackstocks (Tiger River), South Carolina (November 20)		

WINS	LOSSES	INCONCLUSIVE
		Long Cane, South Carolina (December 11)
		Halfway Swamp, Singleton, South Carolina (December 12-13)
Boyd Creek, Tennessee (December 16 – two victories)*		
1781		
Freeland's Fort, Tennessee (January 15)*		
Cowpens, South Carolina (January 17)*		Georgetown, South Carolina (January 24)
	Catawba River, North Carolina (February 1)*	
		Shallow Ford, North Carolina (February 6)
Haw River, North Carolina (February 25)		
Cherokee Towns Destroyed, Tennessee (March)*		
Wiboo Swamp, South Carolina (March 6)		
	Guilford Courthouse, North Carolina (March 15)	
Beatties Mill, South Carolina (March 21)		
		Ft. Nashborough, Tennessee (April 2)*
Ft. Watson, South Carolina (April 15-23)		
Augusta, Georgia (April 16-June 5 – three victories)		
Orangeburg, South Carolina (May 11)		
Ft. Motte, South Carolina (May 12)		
	Siege of "96," South Carolina (June 19)	
Strikes Against Cherokees (June)*		
		Spencer's Tavern, Virginia (June 26)
	Green Springs, Virginia (July 6)	
	Quinby's Bridge, South Carolina (July 17)	
Parker's Ferry, South Carolina (August 13)		
	Lochry's Defeat, Ohio (August 25)*	
	Eutaw Springs, South Carolina (September 8)	
Moccasin Creek, Tennessee (September 11)*		
Yorktown, Virginia (September 29-October 9)		
Fairlawn, South Carolina (November 27)		

WINS	LOSSES	INCONCLUSIVE

1782

WINS	LOSSES	INCONCLUSIVE
Gnadenhuettan Massacre, Ohio (March 7-8)*		
"Navy" Riflemen, Delaware River (April)*		
	Sandusky, Ohio (June 4-5)*	
Bryan's Station, Kentucky (August 15)*		
	Battle Run Branch, Kentucky (August)*	
	Blue Licks, Kentucky (August 19)*	
Ft. Henry, West Virginia (September 11-13)*		
Lookout Mountain, Tennessee (September 20)*		
Chillicothe, Ohio (November 10)*		

FINAL TALLY: ACTIONS IN WHICH RIFLE TROOPS PARTICIPATED

100 (63%)	42 (27%)	16 (10%)

ACTIONS IN WHICH MOST OR ALL AMERICAN COMBATANTS WERE RIFLEMEN

49 (74%)	12 (18%)	4 (7%)

CHAPTER 5

CONTEMPORARY ACCOUNTS OF
THE DRESS, MARKSMANSHIP AND CHARACTER
OF FRONTIER RIFLEMEN

CLOTHING AND ACCOUTREMENTS

". . . Throughout all this country, and in every back settlement in America, the roads and paths are first marked out by blazes on the trees, cut alternately on each side of the way, every thirty or forty yards . . . The convenience and simplicity of this mode has rendered it universal throughout the whole back country.

"It became the more readily adopted, as all who travel beyond the roads and beaten tracks, always have tomahawks in their belts; which, in such situations and circumstances, are more useful than anything, except the rifle-barreled firelocks; both of which all the male inhabitants habituate themselves constantly to carry along with them everywhere.

"Their whole dress is also very singular, and not very materially different from that of the Indians; being a hunting shirt, somewhat resembling a waggoner's frock, ornamented with a great many fringes, tied round the middle with a broad belt, much decorated also, in which is fastened a tomahawk, an instrument that serves every purpose of defense and convenience; being a hammer at one side and a sharp hatchet at the other; the shot bag and powder-horn, carved with a variety of whimsical figures and devices, hang from their necks over one shoulder; and on their heads a flapped hat, of a reddish hue, proceeding from the intensely hot beams of the sun.

"Sometimes they wear leather breeches, made of Indian dressed elk, or deer skins, but more frequently thin trowsers [sic].

"On their legs they have Indian boots, or leggings, made of coarse woolen cloth, that either are wrapped around loosely and tied with garters, or are laced upon the outside, and always come better than half way up the thigh: these are a great defence and preservative, not only against the bite of serpents and poisonous insects, but likewise against the scratches of thorns, briars, scrubby bushes and underwood, with which this whole country is infested and overspread.

"On their feet they sometimes wear pumps of their own manufacture, but generally Indian moccossons [sic], of their own construction also, which are made of strong elk's or buck's skin, dressed soft as for gloves or breeches, drawn together in regular plaits over the toe, and lacing from thence round to the fore part of the middle of the ancle[sic], without a seam in them, yet fitting close to the feet, and are indeed perfectly easy and pliant.

"Thus habited and accoutered, with his rifle upon his shoulder, or in his hand, a back-wood's man is completely equipped for visiting, courtship, travel, hunting or war.

"And according to the number and variety of the fringes on his hunting shirt, and the decorations on his powder-horn, belt and rifle, he estimates his finery, and absolutely conceives himself of equal consequence, more civilized, polite and more elegantly dressed than the most brilliant peer at St. James's in a splendid and expensive birthday suit, of the first fashion and taste, and most costly materials.

"Their hunting, or rifle shirts, they have also died [sic] in variety of colours, some yellow, others red, some brown and many wear them quite white.

"Such sentiments as those I have just exposed to notice, are neither so ridiculous nor surprising, when the circumstances are considered with due attention, that prompt the back-wood's American to such a train of thinking, and in which light it is, that he feels his own consequence, for he finds all his resources in himself.

"Thus attired and accoutered, as already described, set him in the midst of a boundless forest, a thousand miles from an inhabitant, he is by no means at a loss, nor in the smallest degree dismayed.

"With his rifle he procures his subsistence; with his tomahawk he erects his shelter, his wigwam, his house or whatever habitation he may chuse [sic] to reside in; he drinks at the crystal spring, or the nearest brook; his wants are all easily supplied, he is contented, he is happy. For felicity, beyond a doubt, consists, in a great measure, in the attainment and gratification of our desires, and the accomplishment of the utmost bounds of our wishes.

"This digression, which I thought necessary to impress an idea of the singular appearance and sentiments of these men, for that reason, I am hopeful, will be excused; and for which, I flatter myself, this will be deemed a sufficient apology."

J.F.D. Smyth, <u>Tour In The United States of America</u>, 1784.

". . . The uniform of Morgan's Regiment was a short frock made of pepper and salt colored cotton cloth like a common working frock worn by our country people, except that it was short and open before, to be tied with strings; pantaloons of the same fabric and color, and some kind of a cap, but I do not now remember its form. This was their summer dress."

<u>19th Century Pension Papers, Describing Daniel Morgan's Company of Riflemen In 1775.</u>

"Declarant states that he was then stationed at Fort Pitt, the place aforesaid. Declarant states that in obedience to the order of his said Captain Brady, he proceeded to tan his thighs and legs with wild cherry and white oak bark and to equip himself after the following manner, to wit, a breechcloth, leather leggins, moccasins and a cap made out of a racoon skin, with the feathers of a hawk, painted after the manner of an Indian warrior. His face was painted red, with three black stripes across his cheeks, which was a signification of war. Declarant states that Captain Brady's company was about sixty-four in number, all painted after the manner aforesaid."

George Roush, 19th Century Pension Papers, Describing His Clothing In 1777.

"Captain Hugh Stephenson's rendezvous was Shepherd's Town (not Martinsburg) and Captain Morgan's was Winchester. Great exertions were made by each Captain to complete his company first, that merit might be claimed on that account. Volunteers presented themselves in every direction in the vicinity of these towns, none were received but young men of character, and of sufficient property to clothe themselves completely, find their own arms, and accoutrements, that is, an approved rifle, handsome shot pouch and powder horn, blanket, knapsack, with such decent clothing as should be prescribed, but which was at first ordered to be only a hunting shirt and pantaloons, fringed on every edge and in various ways."

Major Henry Bedinger, Letter to a Son Of General Samuel Finley,
Describing The Riflemen Of His Unit In 1775,
written some time later.

". . . I have had the happiness of seeing Captain Michael Cresap marching at the head of a formidable company of upwards of one hundred and thirty men, from the mountains and backwoods, painted like Indians, armed with tomahawks and rifles dressed in hunting shirts and moccasins, and though some of them had traveled near eight hundred miles, from the banks of the Ohio, they seemed to walk light and easy, and not with less spirit than at the first hour of their march. Health and vigor, after what they had undergone, declared them to be intimate with hardship and familiar with danger . . ."

Extract From a Letter to a Gentleman in Philadelphia, 1775.

"Hundreds of backwoodsmen collected at Fredericksburg, Virginia and continued there one or two days longer, should have had upwards of ten thousand men. All the frontier counties were in motion . . . Fredericksburg never was so honored with so many brave hearty men . . . every man rich and poor with their hunting shirts, belts and tomahawks fixed . . . in the best manner."

Michael Wallace, Letter to Gustavius Wallace, 1775.

An eyewitness described the southern riflemen as ". . . Not over-burdened with fat, but tall, raw-boned and sinewy."

Drury Mathis, Loyalist Captured at King's Mountain, 1780.

"The committee appointed me captain of this company of rangers, and gave me the appointment of my subalterns. I chose two of the most active young men that I could find, who had also been long in captivity with the Indians. As we enlisted our men, we dressed them uniformly in the Indian manner, with breech-clouts, leggins, mockesons [sic] and green shrouds, which we wore in the same manner that the Indians do, and nearly as the Highlanders wear their plaids. In place of hats we wore red handerchiefs, and painted our faces red and black, like Indian warriors. I taught them the Indian discipline, as I knew of no other at that time, which would answer the purpose much better than British. We succeeded beyond expectation in defending the frontiers, and were extolled by our employers."

James Smith, Life and Travels of Colonel James Smith, 1799,
describing the dress of his "Black Boys" when formed in the early 1760's.

"Our clothing was all of domestic manufacture. We had no other resource for clothing, and this, indeed, was a poor one. The crops of flax often failed, and the sheep were destroyed by the wolves. Linsey, which is made of flax and wool, the former the chain and the latter the filling, was the warmest and most substantial cloth we could make. Almost every house contained a loom, and almost every woman was a weaver.
"Every family tanned their own leather. The tan vat was a large trough sunk to the upper edge in the ground. A quantity of bark was easily obtained every spring, in clearing and fencing the land. This, after drying, was brought in and in wet days was shaved and pounded on a block of wood, with an axe or mallet. Ashes was [sic] used in place of lime for taking off the hair. Bears' oil, hog's lard and tallow, answered the place of fish oil. The leather, to be sure, was coarse;

but it was substantially good. The operation of currying was performed by a drawing knife with its edge turned, after the manner of a currying knife. The blacking for the leather was made of soot and hog's lard.

"Almost every family contained its own tailors and shoemakers. Those who could not make shoes, could make shoepacks. These, like moccasons [sic], were made of a single piece of leather with the exception of a tongue piece on the top of the foot. This was about two inches broad and circular at the lower end. To this the main piece of leather was sewed, with a gathering stitch. The seam behind was like that of a moccason [sic]. To the shoepack a sole was sometimes added. The women did the tailor work. They could all cut out and make hunting shirts, leggins and drawers."

Reverend Joseph Doddridge, <u>Notes on the Settlements and Indian Wars</u> <u>of the Western Parts of Virginia and Pennsylvania</u>, 1763-1783.

"The principle distinction between us, was in our dialects, our arms and our dress. Each man of the three companies bore a rifle-barreled gun, a tomahawk, or small axe, and a long knife, usually called a 'scalping knife,' which served for all purposes, in the woods. His under-dress, by no means in a military style, was covered by a deep ash-colored hunting shirt, leggins and moccasins, if the latter could be procured. It was the silly fashion of those times for the riflemen to ape the manner of savages . . .

"My wardrobe was scanty and light. It consisted of a roundabout jacket of woolen, a pair of half-worn buckskin breeches, two pairs of woolen stockings, (bought at Newburyport,) a hat with a feather, a hunting shirt, leggins, a pair of mockasins [sic], a pair of tolerably good shoes, which had been closely hoarded . . .

"[George] Merchant was a tall and handsome Virginian. In a few days, he, hunting-shirt and all, was sent to England, probably as a finished specimen of the riflemen of the colonies. The government there very liberally sent him home in the following year . . .

"By-and-by [Daniel] Morgan came, large, a commanding aspect, and stentorian voice. He wore leggins, and a cloth in the Indian style. His thighs, which were exposed to view, appeared to have been lacerated by the thorns and bushes . . .

"My gloves were good and well lined with fur, and my mockasins [sic] of the best kind, well stuffed . . .

"Having on a fine white blanket coat, and turning my cap or 'bonnet rouge' inside out, the inside being white, made me, as it were, invisible in the snow . . .

John Joseph Henry, <u>An Accurate and Interesting Account of the Hardships</u> <u>and Sufferings of That Band of Heroes, Who Traversed Thru The</u> <u>Wilderness in the Campaign Against Quebec in 1775</u>, 1812.

James Smith as an Indian:
"They gave me a new ruffled shirt, which I put on, also a pair of leggins done off with ribbons and beads, likewise a pair of mockasons [sic], and garters dressed with beads, porcupine-quills and red hair – also a tinsel laced cappo. They again painted my head and face with various colors, and tied a bunch of red feathers to one of these locks they had left on the crown of my head, which stood up five or six inches . . .

And Smith as a returning Long Hunter:
"When I came into the settlement my clothes were almost worn out, and the boy had nothing on him that ever was spun. He had buck-skin leggins, mockasons [sic], and breech-clout – a bear-skin dressed with the hair on, which he belted about him, and a raccoon-skin cap . . .

"I went to a magistrate, and obtained a pass, and one of my old acquaintances made me a present of a shirt. I then cast away my old rags, and all the clothes I now had was an old beaver hat, buck-skin leggins, mockasons {sic], and a new shirt; also an old blanket, which I commonly carried on my back in good weather. Being thus equipped, I marched on, with my white shirt loose, and Jamie with his bear-skin about him: – myself appearing white, and Jamie very black, alarmed the dogs where-ever we came, so that they barked violently."

James Smith, <u>An Account of the Remarkable Occurances in the</u> <u>Life and Travels of Colonel James Smith</u>, 1799.

"The people all travel on horseback, with pistols and swords, an a large blanket folded up under their saddle, which last they use for sleeping in when obliged to pass the night in the woods.

"The moccasin is made of the skin of the deer, elk, or buffalo, which is commonly dressed without the hair, and rendered of a deep brown colour by being exposed to the smoke of a wood fire. It is formed of a single piece of leather, with a seam from the toe to the instep, and another behind, similar to that in a common shoe; by means of a thong it is fastened round the instep, just under the ankle-bone, and is thus made to sit very close to the foot. Round that part where the foot is put in, a flap of the depth of an inch or two is left, which hangs loosely down over the string by which the moccasin is fastened; and this flap as also the seam, are tastefully ornamented with porcupine quills and beads: the flap is edged with tin or copper tags filled with scarlet hair, if the moccasin be intended for a man, and with ribbands [sic] if for a woman. An ornamented moccasin of this sort is only worn in dress, as the ornaments are expensive, and the leather soon wears out; one of the plain leather answers for ordinary use. Many of the white people on the Indian frontiers wear this kind of shoe; but a person not accustomed to walk in it, or to walk barefoot, cannot wear it abroad, on a rough road, without great inconvenience, as every unevenness of surface is felt through the leather, which is soft and pliable: in a house it is the most agreeable sort of shoe that can be imagined: Indians wear it universally.

"Above the moccasin all the Indians wear what are called leggings, which reach from the instep to the middle of the thigh. They are commonly made of blue or scarlet cloth, and are formed so as to sit close to the limbs, like the modern pantaloons; but the edges of the cloth annexed to the seam, instead of being turned in, are left on the outside, and are ornamented with beads, ribands [sic], &C., when the leggings are intended for dress. Many of the young warriors are so desirous that their leggings should fit them neatly, that they make the squaws, who are the tailors, and really very good ones, sow [sic] them tight on their limbs, so that they cannot be taken off, and they continue to wear them constantly till they are reduced to rags. The leggings are kept up by means of two strings, one on the outside of each thigh, which are fastened to a third, that is tied around the waist.

"They also wear round the waist another string, from which are suspended two little aprons, somewhat more than a foot square, one hanging down before and the other behind, and under these a piece of cloth, drawn close up to the body between the legs, forming a sort of truss. The aprons and this piece of cloth, which are all fastened together, are called the breech cloth. The utmost ingenuity of the squaws is exerted in adorning the little aprons with beads, ribbands [sic] &C.

"The moccasins, leggings, and breech cloth constitute the whole of the dress which they wear when they enter upon a campaign, except indeed it be a girdle, from which hangs their tobacco pouch and scalping knife, &C; nor do they wear anything more when the weather is very warm; but when it is cool, or when they dress themselves to visit their friends, they put on a short shirt, loose at the neck and wrists, generally made of coarse figured cotton or calico, of some gaudy pattern, not unlike what would be used for window or bed curtains at a common inn in England. Over the shirt they wear either a blanket, large piece of broad cloth, or else a loose coat made somewhat similarly to a common riding frock; a blanket is more commonly worn than anything else. They tie one end of it round their waste [sic] with a girdle, and then drawing it over their shoulders, either fasten it across their breasts with a skewer, or hold the corners of it together, in the left hand. One would imagine that this last mode of wearing it could not but be highly inconvenient to them, as it must deprive them in a great measure of the use of one hand; yet it is the mode in which it is commonly worn, even when they are shooting in the woods; they generally, however, keep the right arm disengaged when they carry a gun, and draw the blanket over the left shoulder."

Isaac Weld, Travels Through the States Of North America, 1799.

"You expressed apprehension that the rifle dress of General Morgan may be mistaken hereafter for a waggoner's frock, which he, perhaps, wore when on the expedition with General Braddock; there is no more resemblence between the two dresses, than between a cloak and a coat; the waggoner's frock was intended, as the present cartman's to cover and protect their other clothes, and is merely a long coarse shirt reaching below the knee; the dress of the Virginia riflemen who came to Cambridge in 1775 [among whom was Morgan] was an elegant loose dress reaching to the middle of the thigh, ornamented with fringes in various parts and meeting the pantaloons of the same material and color, fringed and ornamented in corresponding style. The officers wore the usual crimson sash over this, and around the waist, the straps, belts, etc. were black, forming, in my opinion, a very picturesque and elegant as well as useful dress. It cost a trifle; the soldier could wash it at any brook he passed; however worn and ragged and dirty his other clothing might be, when this was thrown over it, he was in elegant uniform."

John Trumbull, Personal Letter, circa 1780.

"Leggers, leggins, or Indian spatterdashes, are usually made of frieze or other coarse woolen cloth; they should be at least three quarters wide (which is 3 x 3) then double it, and sew it together from end to end, within four, five or six inches of the outside selvages, fitting this long narrow bag to the shape of the leg; the flaps to be on the outside, which serve to wrap over the skin, or forepart of the leg, tied round under the knee, and above the ankle, with garters of the same colour; by which the legs are preserved from many fatal accidents, in marching through the woods. The Indians generally ornament the flaps with beads of various colours, as they do their moggasan [sic], for my part, I think them clumsy, and not at all military; yet I confess they are highly necessary in N. America; nevertheless, if they were made without the flap and to button the outside of the leg, in like manner as a spatterdash they would answer full as well: but this is a matter of opinion."

Captain John Knox, Historical Journal, 1757.

"At the head of the column marched a group of woodsmen, all of course, bearing rifles. Some strode on foot but many of them, perhaps the majority, were mounted on horses that walked slowly along.

"They wore loose hunting shirts, and trousers of dressed deerskin, gayley [sic] decorated with the colored fringes so widely affected as a backwoods fashion. Their feet were clad in moccasins and on their heads were many sorts of fantastic caps of skins or of linsey woolsey, each fashioned according the whim of its owner. Every man was girt with a leather belt from the right side of which hung a tomahawk to be used either as a hatchet or for some more violent purpose. On his left side he carried his hunting knife, a full powder horn, a leather pouch of home made bullets and another large leather pouch holding a quart or two of parched corn."

Anonymous <u>Description of a Party of Long Hunters</u>, 1773.

"I am of opinion that a number of hunting-shirts, not less than ten thousand, would in a great degree remove this difficulty, in the cheapest and quickest manner. I know nothing in a speculative view, more trivial, yet which, if put in practice, would have a happier tendency to unite the men, and abolish those provincial distinctions that lead to jealousy and dissatisfaction."

George Washington, <u>Letter to the President of Congress</u>, 1775.

"Hunting shirts with long breeches . . . it is a dress justly supposed to carry no small terror to the enemy who think every such person a complete marksman."

George Washington, July, 1776.

Nicholas Cresswell recalled that his companions on a journey along the Kentucky River had not two pairs of breeches among them. "The rest wear breechclouts, leggins and hunting shirts, which have never been washed, only by the rain since they were made.

"It is a custom with our company, as soon as it begins to rain to strip naked and secure their clothes from the wet. I have attempted it twice today, but the drops of rain are disagreeable to my skin, that it obliged me to put on my shirt." Cresswell noted that the frontier was "an asylum for rascals of all denominations."

<u>Journal of Nicholas Cressell</u>, 1774-1777.

"The Indians, who have any dealings with the English or American traders, and all of them have that live in the neighborhood, and to the east of the Mississippi, and in the neighborhood of the great lakes to the north-west, have now totally laid aside the use of furs and skins in their dress, except for their shoes or moccasins, and sometimes for their leggins, as they find they can exchange them to advantage for blankets and woolen cloths, &C. which they consider likewise as much more agreeable and commodious materials for wearing apparel."

Isaac Weld, <u>Travels Through the States of North America</u>, 1799.

"On the frontiers, and particularly amongst those who were much in the habit of hunting, and going on scouts and campaigns, the dress of the men was partly Indian, and partly that of civilized nations.

"The hunting shirt was universally worn. This was a kind of loose frock, reaching halfway down the thighs, with large sleeves, open before and so wide as to lap over a foot or more when belted. The cape was large, and sometimes handsomely fringed with a ravelled piece of cloth of a different color from that of the hunting shirt itself. The bosom of this dress served as a wallet to hold a chunk of bread, cakes, jerk, tow for wiping the barrel of the rifle, or any other necessary for the hunter or warrior.

"The belt, which was always tied behind answered several purposes, besides that of holding the dress together. In cold weather the mittens, and sometimes the bullet-bag, occupied the front part of it. To the right side was suspended the tomahawk and to the left the scalping knife in its leather sheath. The hunting shirt was generally made of linsey, sometimes of coarse linen, and a few of dressed deer skins. These last were very cold and uncomfortable in wet weather. The shirt and jacket were of the common fashion. A pair of drawers or breeches and leggins, were the dress of the thighs and legs; a pair of moccasons [sic] answered for the feet much better than shoes. These were made of dressed deer skin. They were mostly made of a single piece with a gathering seam along the top of the foot, and another from the bottom of the heel, without gathers as high as the ankle joint or a little higher. Flaps were left on each side to reach some distance up the legs. These were nicely adapted to the ankles, and, lower part of the leg by thongs of deer skin, so that no dust, gravel, or snow could get within the moccason [sic].

"The moccasons [sic] in ordinary use cost but a few hours labor to make them. This was done by an instrument denominated a moccason [sic] awl, which was made of the backspring of an old claspknife. This awl with its buckhorn handle was an appendage of every shot pouch strap, together with a roll of buckskin for mending the moccasons [sic]. This was the labor of almost every evening. They were sewed together and patched with deer skin thongs, or whangs, as they were commonly called.

"In cold weather the moccasons [sic] were well stuffed with deer's hair or dry leaves, so as to keep the feet comfortably warm; but in wet weather it was usually said that wearing them was 'a decent way of going barefooted,' and such was the fact, owing to the spongy texture of the leather of which they were made.

"Owing to this defective covering of the feet, more than to any other circumstance, the greater number of our hunters and warriors were afflicted with the rheumatism in their limbs. Of this disease they were all apprehensive in cold or wet weather, and therefore always slept with their feet to the fire to prevent or cure it as well as they could. This practice unquestionably had a very salutary effect, and prevented many of them from becoming confirmed cripples in early life.

"In the latter years of the Indian war our young men became more enamored of the Indian dress throughout, with the exception of the matchcoat. The drawers were laid aside and the leggins made longer, so as to reach the upper part of the thigh. The Indian breech clout was adopted. This was a piece of linen or cloth nearly a yard long, and eight or nine inches broad. This passed under the belt before and behind leaving the end for flaps hanging before and behind over the belt. The flaps were sometimes ornamented with some coarse kind of embroidery work. To the same belt which secured the breech clout, strings which supported the long leggins were attached. When this belt, as was often the case, passed over the hunting shirt the upper part of the thighs and part of the hips were naked.

"The young warrior instead of being abashed by this nudity was proud of his Indian like dress. In some few instances I have seen them go into places of public worship in this dress. Their appearance, however, did not add much to the devotion of the young ladies."

Reverend Joseph Doddridge, <u>Notes on the Settlements and Indian Wars
of the Western Parts of Virginia and Pennsylvania 1763-1783.</u>

"Boone was dressed in deer-skin colored black, and had his hair plaited and clubbed up..."

Daniel Trabue, remembering Daniel Boone and how
he was clothed in 1773, during the latter's longhunter
days. It would appear that many of these men,
whether out of choice or through necessity, chose to
wear buckskin when so far from the settlements.

MARKSMANSHIP AND EFFECTIVENESS

"Colonel, now General, Tarleton, and myself, were standing a few yards out of a wood, observing the situation of a part of the enemy which we intended to attack. There was a rivulet in the enemy's front, and a mill on it, to which we stood directly with horses' heads fronting, observing their motions. It was absolutely a plain field between us and the mill; not so much as a single bush on it. Our orderly-bugler stood behind us about three yards, but with his horse's side to our horses' tails. A rifleman passed over the milldam, evidently observing two officers, and laid himself down on his belly; for in such positions they always lie, to take a good shot at a long distance. He took a deliberate and cool shot at my friend, at me; and at the bugle-horn man. Now observe how well this fellow shot. It was in the month of August, and not a breath of wind was stirring. Colonel Tarleton's horse and mine, I am certain, were not anything like two feet apart; for we were in close consultation, how we should attack with our troops which laid 300 yards in the wood, and could not be perceived by the enemy. A rifle-ball passed between him and me; looking directly to the mill I evidently observed the flash of the powder. I directly said to my friend, 'I think we had better move, or we shall have two or three of these gentlemen shortly amusing themselves at our expense.' The words were hardly out of my mouth when the bugle-horn man behind me, and directly central, jumped off his horse and said, 'Sir, my horse is shot.' The horse staggered, fell down, and died . . . Now speaking of this rifleman's shooting, nothing could be better . . . I have passed several times over this ground and ever observed it with the greatest attention; and I can positively assert that the distance he fired from at us was full 400 yards."

Colonel George Hanger, <u>To All Sportsmen and Particularly to Farmers and Gamekeepers</u>, 1814.

"They are remarkable at Philadelphia for making rifled Barrell Gunns, [sic] which throw a Ball above 300 yards, vastly well, & much better than any other Barrells. People here in general Shoot very well with Ball, but don't doe [sic] much with Shot."

<u>Sir William Johnson Papers</u>, 1761.

"A large part of the provincials are armed with grooved rifles, and have their molds. Lead in bars will suit them better than bullets – likewise the Indians –, but they also need fine powder FF."

Colonel Henry Bouquet, <u>Carlisle, Pennsylvania</u>, 1758.

"On Friday evening last arrived here, on their way to the American Camp, Captain (Michael) Cresap's Company of Riflemen, consisting of 130 active, brave young fellows; many of whom had been in the late expedition under Lord Dunmore, against the Indians. They bear in their bodies visible marks of their prowess, and show scars and wounds, which would do honour to Homer's Iliad, etc. They shew[sic] you, to use the poet's words –
'Where the goar'd bull bled at every vein.'
" 'One of these warriors, in particular, shows the cicatrices (scar tissue) of four bullet holes through his body. These men have been bred in the woods to hardships and danger from their infancy. They appear as if they were entirely unacquainted with, and had never felt, the passion of fear. With their rifles in their hands they assume a kind of omnipotence over their enemies. You will not much wonder at this when I mention a fact, which can be fully attested by several of the reputable inhabitants of this place, who were eyewitnesses of it. Two brothers in the company took a piece of board, five inches broad, and seven inches long, with a bit of white paper, about the size of a dollar, nailed in the center, and while one them supported this board perpendicularly between his knees, the other at the distance of upwards of sixty yards, and without any kind of rest, shot eight bullets successively through the board, and spared a brother's thighs!
'Another of the company held a barrel stave perpendicularly in his hand, with one edge close to his side, while one of his comrades at the same distance, and in the manner before mentioned, shot several bullets through it, without any apprehensions of danger on either side. The spectators, appearing to be amazed at these feats, were told that there were upwards of fifty persons in the company who could do the same thing; that there was not one who could not plug 19 bullets out of 20 (as they termed it) within an inch of the head of a ten-penny nail; in short, to evince the confidence they possessed in their dexterity at these kinds of arms, some of them proposed to stand with apples on their heads, while others at the same distance undertook to shoot them off; but the people who saw the other experiments, declined to be witnesses of this. At night a great fire was kindled round a pole planted in the courthouse square, where the company with the Captain at their head, all naked to the waist and painted like savages (except the Captain, who was in an Indian shirt), indulged a vast concourse of the inhabitants with a perfect exhibition of a war

dance, and all the manoeuvres [sic] of Indians holding council, going to war, circumventing their enemies, by defiles, ambuscades, attacking, scalping, etc. It is said by those who are judges, that no representation could possibly come nearer the original. The Captain's agility and expertness, in particular, in these exhibitions, astonished every beholder.

'This morning they will set out on their march to Cambridge'."

Pennsylvania Packet, August, 1775 Lancaster, Pennsylvania

"Yesterday the company was supplied with a small quantity of powder from the magazine, which wanted airing, and was not in good order for rifles; in the evening, however, they were drawn out to show the gentlemen of the Town their dexterity at shooting. A clapboard, with a mark the size of a dollar, was put up; they began to fire offhand, and the bystanders were surprised, few shots being made that were not close to or in the paper. When they had shot for a time in this way, some lay on their back, some on their breast or side, others ran twenty or thirty steps, and firing appeared to be equally certain of the mark. With this performance the company was more than satisfied, when a young man took up the board in his hand, not by the end, but by the side, and holding it as it was held before, the second brother shot as the former had done. By this exercise I was more astonished than pleased. But will you believe me when I tell you, that one of the men took the board, and placing it between his legs, stood with his back to the tree while another drove the center. What would a regular army of considerable strength in the forests of America do with one thousand of these men, who want nothing to preserve their health and courage but water from the spring, with a little parched corn, with what they can easily procure in hunting; and who, wrapped in their blankets, in the damp of night, would choose the shade of a tree for their covering, and the earth for their bed?"

Extract of a Letter to a Gentleman in Philadelphia, Describing a Shooting Match Held by Captain Michael Cresap's Company of Riflemen, 1775.

"The inhabitants of Red Bank are only hunters, or what are called foresters. They cultivate no ground, but subsist on the produce of their hunting and fishing, and are almost naked. The following trait may serve to give an idea of their character. At our arrival we found a number of these hunters who had assembled to regale themselves on the banks of the river with the spoils of their chace [sic] on the preceeding day, when they had killed a very fine buffalo. They had drunk plentifully of whiskey, and though the greater number were intoxicated, they were amusing themselves in firing with carabines [sic] against a piece of plank tied to a tree, which is called shooting at a mark. The board, probably ill-fastened, fell at each shot; one of the party at length losing patience, took it up, and placing it between his legs, called out to his companion, 'Now fire away!' which they did immediately, and always with the same address; whilst he who held the board exclaimed at each shot, 'It is in!' This amusement, which lasted two hours without any accident taking place, may appear incredible to those who are not acquainted with the singular skill of these men; but it is sufficient to observe that they will aim at the head of a squirrel or a turkey and very rarely miss. The seeming intrepidity of the man who held the board becomes, therefore, only an ordinary circumstance."

General Victor Callot, 1796.

"Their guns are rifled barrels, and they fight in ambush, five hundred provincials would stop the march of five thousand regulars. And a whole army might be cut off, without knowing where the fire came from."

Gentleman's Magazine, 1775.

"I have many times asked the American backwoodsman what was the most their best marksmen could do; they have constantly told me that an expert rifleman, provided he can draw good and true sight, can hit the head of a man at 200 yards. I am certain that provided an American rifleman was to get a perfect aim at 300 yards at me standing still, he most undoubtedly would hit me, unless it was a very windy day . . ."

Colonel George Hanger, To All Sportsmen and Particularly to Farmers and Gamekeepers, 1814.

". . . they apprehend a Rifleman grows naturally behind each Tree and Bush on the Continent."

Captain Thomas Pinckney, Commenting on the British Fear of Riflemen, 1775.

At one time, Thomas Jefferson advised Lafayette to retreat to the west so that the British would be exposed ". . . to their most dangerous Enemies, the Riflemen."

Thomas Jefferson, Letter to the Marquis de Lafayette, 1781.

Well into the war, the commander-in-chief still believed that a ". . . corps of riflemen will be for several purposes extremely useful."

George Washington, Letter to the Secretary of War, 1778.

"Let us take a view of the benefits we have received, by what little we have learned of their [Indian] art of war, which cost us dear, and the loss that we have sustained for want of it; and then see if it will not be well worth our while to retain what we have, and also to endeavor to improve in this necessary branch of business. Though we have made considerable proficiency in this line, and in some respects out-do them viz. as marksmen, and in cutting our rifles, and in keeping them in good order; yet, I apprehend we are far behind in their manoeuveres, or in being able to surprize [sic], or prevent a surprize [sic]. May we not conclude that the progress we had made in their art of war contributed considerably towards our success, in various respects, when contending with Great Britain for liberty?

"Had the British King, attempted to enslave us before Braddock's war, in all probability he might readily have done it, because, except the New Englanders, who had formerly been engaged in war with the Indians, we were unacquainted with any kind of war: but after fighting such a subtil [sic] and barbarous enemy as the Indians, we were not terrified at the approach of British red-coats. – Was not Burgoyne's defeat accomplished in some measure by the Indian mode of fighting? and did not Gen. Morgan's rifle-men, and many others, fight with greater success, in consequence of what they had learned of their art of war? Kentucky would not have been settled at the time it was, had the Virginians been altogether ignorant of this method of war."

Colonel James Smith, An Account of the Remarkable Ocurances in the Life and Travels of Colonel James Smith, 1799.

"The fire was now return'd, but the enemy had a great advantage from their rifles . . ."

Colonel Henry Hamilton, 1779, describing his defense of Fort Sackville in the Illinois Country.

"I cannot sufficiently thank your Excellency for sending Col. Morgan's corps to this army; they shall be of the greatest service to it . . ."

General Horatio Gates, Letter to George Washington, 1777, during the Saratoga campaign.

"They either did not or would not take the signal; and though there were but two of us, from whom they could not possibly expect a design to attack, they did not cease firing at us. I may venture to say, that not less than ten guns were discharged with their muzzles towards us, within the distance of forty or fifty yards, and I might be nearer the truth in saying, that some were let off within twenty. Luckily for us, it was not our riflemen to whom we were targets . . ."

Alexander Graydon, Commenting on the Ineffectiveness of British Muskets in Battle, 1776.

"An unusual number of the killed were found to have been shot in the head. Riflemen took off riflemen with such exactness, that they killed each other when they were taking sight, so effactually that their eyes remained after they were dead, one shut and the other open, in the usual manner of marksmen when leveling at their subjects."

A Loyalist's Description of Riflemen at King's Mountain, 1780.

"Shooting at marks was a common diversion among the men, when their stock of ammunition would allow it;

this, however, was far from being always the case. The present mode of shooting off hand was not then in practice. This mode was not considered as any trial of the value of a gun; nor, indeed, as much of a test of the skill of a marksmen. Their shooting was from a rest, and at as great a distance as the length and weight of the barrel of the gun would throw a ball on a horizontal level. Such was their regard to accuracy, in these supportive trials of their rifles, and of their own skill in the use of them, that they often put moss, or some other soft substance, on the log or stump from which they shot, for fear of having the bullet thrown from the mark by the spring of the barrel. When the rifle was held to the side of a tree for a rest, it was pressed against it as lightly as possible, for the same reason.

"Rifles of former times, were different from those of modern date; few of them carried more than forty-five bullets (.47 caliber) to the pound. Bullets of a less size were not thought sufficiently heavy for hunting or war."

Reverend Joseph Doddridge,
Notes on the Settlements and Indian Wars of the
Western Parts of Virginia and Pennsylvania, 1763-1783.

"In consequence of the orders of His Excellency Gen'l Washington, I now send Major Miller for arms and clothing for the First Pennsylvania Regiment commanded by Colonel Chambers; they never received any uniforms, except hunting shirts, which were worn out and although a body of fine men, yet from being in rags and badly armed, they are viewed with contempt by the other troops, and began to despise themselves. The conduct of the Pennsylvanians the other day, in forcing General Grant to retire with circumstances of shame and disgrace into the very lines of the enemy, has gained them the esteem and confidence of His Excellency, who wishes to have our rifles exchanged for good muskets and bayonets, as experience has taught us they are not fit for the field, and a few only will be retained in each regiment which will be placed in the hands of real marksmen."

General Anthony Wayne, Letter to the Board of War, 1777.

Interestingly, while Wayne acknowledged the victory of the riflemen, he also believed their arms to be inferior. The following year he issued an order to ". . . 'make a return of the number of Rifles in each Brigade, in order to Exchange them for an equal number of Muskets and Bayonets'."

General Anthony Wayne, 2nd Pennsylvania Regiment's Orderly Book, 1778.

"Several different kinds of articles are manufactured at Lancaster by German mechanics, individually, principally for the people of the town and the neighbourhood. Rifled barrel guns however are to be excepted, which, although not as handsome as those imported from England, are more esteemed by the hunters, and are sent to every part of the country.

"The rifled barrel guns, commonly used in America, are nearly of the length of a musket, and carry leaden balls from the size of thirty to sixty in the pound (from .53 to .42 caliber). Some hunters prefer those of a small bore, because they require but little ammunition; others prefer such as have a wide bore, because the wound which they inflict is more certainly attended with death; the wound, however, made by a ball discharged from one of these guns, is always very dangerous. The inside of the barrel is fluted, and the grooves run in a spiral direction from one end of the barrel to the other, consequently when the ball comes out it has a whirling motion round its own axis, at the same time that it moves forward, and when it enters into the body of an animal, it tears up the flesh in a dreadful manner. The best of powder is chosen for the rifled barrel gun, and after a proper portion of it is put down the barrel, the ball is inclosed [sic] in a small bit of linen rag, well greased at the outside, and then forced down with a thick ramrod. The grease and the bits of rag, which are called patches, are carried in a little box at the but-end [sic] of the gun. The best rifles are furnished with two triggers, one of which being first pulled sets the other, that is, alters the spring so that it will yield even to the slight touch of a feather. They are also furnished with double sights along the barrel, as fine as those of a surveying instrument. An experienced marksman, with one of these guns, will hit an object not larger than a crown piece, to a certainty, at the distance of one hundred yards. Two men belonging to the Virginia rifle regiment, a large division of which was quartered in this down [sic] during the war, had such a dependance on each other's dexterity, that the one would hold a piece of board, not more than nine inches square, between his knees, whilst the other shot at it with a ball at the distance of one hundred paces. This they used to do alternately, for the amusement of the town's people, as often as they were called upon. Numbers of people in Lancaster can vouch for the truth of this fact. Were I, however, to tell you all the stories I have heard of the performance of riflemen, you would think the people were most abominably addicted to lying. A rifle gun will not carry shot, nor will it carry a ball much farther than one hundred yards with certainty."

Isaac Weld, Travels Through the States of North America, 1799.

"Rifle Men that for their number make the most formidable light infantry in the world. The six frontier countries (of Virginia) can produce 6000 of these Men (with) their amazing hardihood, their method of living so long in the woods without carrying provisions with them, the exceeding quickness with which they can march to distant parts, and above all, the dexterity to which they have arrived in the use of the Rifle Gun. Their [sic] is not one of these Men who wish a distance less than 200 yards or a larger object than an Orange – Every shot is fatal."

Richard Henry Lee, Personal Letter, 1775.

"Sirs: I am favor'd with yours of the 16th. The Spears have come to hand, and are very handy and will be useful to the Rifle Men. But they would be more conveniently carried, if they had a sling fixed to them, they should also have a spike in the but end [sic] to fix them in the ground and they would then serve as a rest for the Rifle. The Iron plates which fix the spear head to the shaft, should be at least eighteen inches long to prevent the Shaft from being cut through, with a stroke of a Horseman's Sword. Those only intended for the Rifle Men, should be fixed with Slings and Spikes in the end, those for the Light Horse need neither. There will be 500 wanting for the Rifle Men, as quick as possible."

George Washington, Letter to the Board of War, 1777.

"I have formed two companies of grenadiers to each regiment, and with spears of 13 feet long. Their rifle (for they are all riflemen) slung over their shoulders, their appearance is formidable, and the men are conciliated to the weapon. I am likewise furnishing myself with four-ounced rifle-amusettes, which will carry an infernal distance; the two-ounced hit a half-sheet of paper 500 yards distant."

Charles Lee, Letter to George Washington, 1776.

Riflemen picked off Tories, too, at Saratoga: "This misfortune accelerated their estrangement from our course and army."

Sergeant Roger Lamb, British Soldier, 1777.

"In the open field the rebels do not count for much, but in the woods, they are formidable."

A Brunswicker, 1777.

As for the Indians at Saratoga: ". . . not a man of them was to be brought in within the sound of a rifle shot."

British Officer, Conduct of the Canada Campaign, 1777.

"These [rebel riflemen] . . . hovered upon the flanks in small detachments, and were very expert in securing themselves, and in shifting the ground . . . many placed themselves in high trees in the rear of their own line, and there was seldom a minute's interval in any part of our line without officers being taken off by a single shot."

General John Burgoyne, State of the Expedition, 1777
[Surrender of Burgoyne at Saratoga, October, 1777].

" . . . their rifle-barrel guns with a ball slit almost in four quarters, when fired out of those guns breaks into four pieces, and generally does great execution."

Virginia Gazette, 1775.

"The Americans load their rifle-barrel guns with a ball slit almost in four quarters, which, when fired out of those guns, breaks in four pieces and generally does great execution."

London Chronicle, 1775.

"I cannot help mentioning one thing, which seems to show the hellish disposition of the accursed rebels: by parcels of ammunition which were left on the field, their balls were all found to be poisoned."

A Loyalist Merchant, Boston, 1775.

"No man could stand at the helm in safety; if the men went aloft to band the sails, they were immediately singled out."

Action Off Hampton Roads, Virginia, 1775,
where riflemen fired upon the enemy from the shore.

" . . . the Riflemen had in one day killed 10 men of a reconnoitering party, and it is said they have killed three officers. A sentry was killed at 250 yards distance."

Pennsylvania Gazette,
Reporting news from the siege of Boston in 1775.

[The] " . . . shirt-tail men, with their cursed twisted guns, the most fatal widow-and-orphan-makers in the world."

London Newspaper, 1775.

"The express, who was sent by the Congress, is returned here from the Eastward, and says he left the Camp last Saturday; that the riflemen picked off ten men in one day, three of whom were Field-officers that were reconnoitering; one of them was killed at the distance of 250 yards, when only half his head was seen."

Pennsylvania Packet, 1775.

A riflemen had killed from a distance of 400 yards to which was added "take care, ministerial troops."

Virginia Gazette, 1775.

"Lord Dunmore, it is said, is much afraid of the riflemen, and has all his vessels caulked up on the sides, above men's height."

Edmund Pendleton, Letter to Richard Henry Lee, 1775.

"The time for which the riflemen enlisted will expire July 1st, and as the loss of such a valuable and brave body of men will be of great injury to the service, I would submit to the consideration of Congress whether it would not be best to adopt some method to induce them to continue. They are indeed a very useful corps; but I need not mention this, as their importance is already well known to the Congress."

George Washington, Letter to the President of Congress, 1776.

"It is a certain truth, that the enemy entertain a most fortunate apprehension of American riflemen. It is equally certain that nothing can contribute to diminish this apprehension so infallibly as a frequent ineffectual fire. It is with some concern, therefore, that I am informed that your men have been suffered to fire at a most preposterous distance. Upon this principle I must entreat and insist that you consider it as a standing order, that not a man under your command is to fire at a greater distance than an hundred and fifty yards, at the utmost; in short, that they never fire without almost a moral certainty of hitting their object."

General Charles Lee, Letter to Colonel William Thompson, 1775.

"At the distance, perhaps, of one hundred and fifty yards, nothing but his head above water, a shooting-match took place, and believe me, the balls of Morgan, Simpson, Humphreys, and others, played around, and within a few inches of his head . . ."

John Joseph Henry, <u>Campaign Against Quebec</u>, 1812, indicating that these rifle officers also used longarms.

Riflemen "can hit a man if within 250 yards, and his head if within 150."

<u>Virginia Gazette</u>, 1775.

"A gentleman from the American camp says – 'Last Wednesday, some riflemen, on Charlestown side, shot an officer of note in the ministerial service, supposed to be Major Small, or Bruce, and killed three men on board a ship at Charlestown ferry, at the distance of full half a mile,'" [800 yards!?!]

<u>Pennsylvania Gazette</u>, 1775.

"The provincials have not a rifleman among them, not one being yet arrived from the southward; nor have they any rifle guns; they have only common muskets, nor are these in general furnished with bayonets; but then, they are almost all marksmen, being accustomed to sporting of one kind or other from their youth."

Dr. William Gordon, <u>Personal Letter</u>, 1775.

[It is] ". . .an unfair method of carrying on a war."

William Carter, <u>British Soldier</u>, 1775, expressing the typical redcoat opinion of the use of rifles in warfare.

[They] ". . . do execution with their rifle guns at an amazing distance."

Warren Adams, <u>Personal Letter</u>, 1775.

"They are grown so terrible to the regulars that nothing is to be seen over the breastwork but a hat."

Dr. Joseph Reed, <u>Personal Letter</u>, 1775.

"Maryland, December 20, 1775 . . . Rifles, infinitely better than those imported, are daily made in many places in Pennsylvania, and all the gunsmiths everywhere constantly employed. In this country, my lord, the boys, as soon as they can discharge a gun, frequently exercise themselves therewith, some a-fowling and others a-hunting. The great quantities of game, the many kinds and the great privileges of killing, making the Americans the best marksmen in the world, and thousands support their families principally by the same, particularly riflemen on the frontiers, whose objects are deer and turkeys. In marching through woods, one thousand of these riflemen would cut to pieces ten thousand of your best troops."

<u>A Minister of the Church of England to the Earl of Dartmouth</u>, 1775.

"This province has raised 1,000 riflemen, the worse of whom will put a ball into a man's head at the distance of 150 to 200 yards; therefore, advise your officers who shall hereafter come out to America to settle their affairs before their departure."

<u>London Chronicle</u>, 1775.

"In this situation Your Excellency would not wish me to part with the corps the army of General Burgoyne are most afraid of."

General Horatio Gates, <u>Letter to George Washington,</u>
<u>in Reference to Morgan's Riflemen,</u> 1777.

"'... [They have] rifles pecularily adapted to take off the officers of a whole line as it marches to an attack,' and that each rifleman was attended by two men to load for him, 'and this is the real cause of so many of our brave officers falling, they being singled out by these murderers, as they must appear to be in the eyes of every thinking man.'"

London Chronicle, 1775.

"A party of these men at a late review on a quick advance, placed their balls in poles of 7 inches diameter, fixed for that purpose, at the distance of 250 yards."

London Chronicle, 1775.

"Sir, you command the finest regiment in the world."

General John Burgoyne, Words Reputedly Spoken to Colonel Daniel Morgan, 1777.

"August ... Several companies of riflemen, amounting, it is said to more than 1400 men, have arrived here from Philadelphia and Maryland, a distance of from 500 to 700 miles. They are remarkably stout and hardy men; many of them exceeding 6 feet in height. They are dressed in white frocks, or rifle shirts, and round hats. These men are remarkable for the accuracy of their aim; striking a mark with great certainty at 200 yards distance. At a review, a company of them, while on a quick advance, fired their balls into objects of 7 inches diameter, at the distance of 250 yards. They are now stationed on our lines, and their shot have frequently proved fatal to British officers and soldiers who expose themselves to view, even at more than double the distance of common musket shot."

Dr. James Thatcher, Military Journal During the American Revolutionary War, 1775.

"... about twilight is found the best season for hunting the rebels in the woods, at which time their rifles are of very little use; and they are not found so serviceable in a body as musketry, a rest being requisite at all times, and before they are able to make a second discharge, it frequently happens that they find themselves run through the body by the push of bayonet, as a rifleman is not entitled to any quarter."

Middlesex Journal, 1776.

"... meeting a corps of rifle-men, namely riflemen only, I would treat them the same as my friend Colonel Abercrombie ... treated Morgan's riflemen. When Morgan's riflemen came down to Pennsylvania from Canada, flushed with success gained over Burgoyne's army, they marched to attack our light infantry, under Colonel Abercrombie. The moment they appeared before him he ordered his troops to charge them with the bayonet; not one man out of four had time to fire, and those that did had no time given them to load again; the light infantry not only dispersed them instantly but drove them for miles over the country. They never attacked, or even looked at, our light infantry again without a regular force to support them."

Colonel George Hanger, To All Sportsmen and Particularly
to Farmers and Gamekeeperse 1814,
evidently referring to the action at Whitemarsh, December 7,1777.
This account is not vouched for in any other contemporary description of that battle.

"Riflemen as riflemen only, are a very feeble foe and not to be trusted alone any distance from camp; and at the outposts they must ever be supported by regulars, or they will constantly be beaten in, and compelled to retire."

Colonel George Hanger, To All Sportsmen and Particularly
to Farmers and Gamekeepers, 1814.

"The riflemen, however dexterous in the use of their arm, were by no means the most formidable of the rebel troops; their not being armed with bayonets, permitted their opponents to take liberties with them which otherwise would have been highly improper."

Lieutenant Colonel John Simcoe,
Simcoe's Military Journal, New York, 1844.

"If muskets were given them instead of rifles the service would be more benefitted, as there is a superabundance of riflemen in the Army. Were it in the power of Congress to supply musketts [sic] they would speedily reduce the number of rifles and replace them with the former, as they are more easily kept in order, can be fired oftener and have the advantage of Bayonetts [sic]."

Richard Peters, <u>Letter to the Council of Safety</u>, 1776.

"The inhabitants of the Ohio country in general have very little of that unmeaning politeness, which we so much praise and admire in the Atlantic States. They are as yet the mere children of nature, and neither their virtues nor their vices are calculated to please refined tastes. They are brave, generous, and humane, and, in proportion to the population, are able to produce the most effective military force of any in our country.

"This preeminence may chiefly be attributed to their exposed situation on an Indian frontier, where they were not only kept in constant danger and alarm, but even found it necessary to teach their sons and daughters, as soon as they were big enough to raise a gun, to load and level the rifle. On more than one occasion have I seen these Spartan females, while engaged at the spinning wheel, or in some other domestic occupation, snatch up the loaded rifle, and fell the bounding deer as he incautiously passed within shot of the cabin. But since peace has been established with the Indians, (most of whom have removed to a greater distance from the whites,) the rifle has become the target of honour among these hardy Americans; and a Kentuckian would scorn to shoot a squirrel, or even a swallow, unless with a rifle; in the choice of which they are even more particular than in selecting a wife. There are a number of rifle manufactories established in this country, but the best and handsomest I have seen are to be procured in Kentucky and Tennessee, where they are made of every size from twenty balls (.61 caliber) to the pound up to one hundred (.36 caliber), and the price from fifteen to a hundred dollars."

Christian Schultz, <u>Travels on an Inland Voyage</u>, 1810.

"These Americans had riflemen - they could hit a man anywhere they liked at two hundred paces distance. We came to dread them far more than the regular Continentals. At Kings Mountain they destroyed us."

<u>Memoirs of Prevost,</u> an English Captain, 1802

84

CHARACTERISTICS AND BEHAVIOR

"A day or two preceeding the incident I am about to relate, a rifle corps had come into camp from Virginia, made up of recruits from the backwoods and mountains of that state, in a uniform dress totally different from that of the regiments raised on the seaboard and interior of New England. Their white linen frocks, ruffled and fringed, excited the curiosity of the whole army, particularly . . . the Marblehead regiment, who were always full of fun and mischief. {They] looked with scorn on such an rustic uniform when compared to their own round jackets and fishers' trousers, [and they] directly confronted from fifty to an hundred of the riflemen who were viewing the college buildings. Their first manifestations were ridicule and derision, which the riflemen bore with more patience than their wont, but resort being made to snow, which then covered the ground, these soft missives were interchanged but a few minutes before both parties closed, and a fierce struggle commenced with biting and gouging on the one part, and knockdown on the other part with as much apparent fury as the most deadly enmity could create. Reinforced by their friends, in less than five minutes more than a thousand combatants were on the field, struggling for the mastery.

"At this juncture, General Washington made his appearance, whether by accident or design I never knew. I only saw him and his colored servant, both mounted. With the spring of a deer, he leaped from his saddle, threw the reins of his bridle into the hands of his servant, and rushed into the thickest of the melee, with an iron grip seized two tall, brawney, athletic, savage-looking riflemen by the throat, keeping them at arm's length, alternately shaking and talking to them. In this position, the eye of the belligerents caught sight of the general. Its effect on them was instantaneous flight at the top of their speed in all directions from the scene of the conflict. Less than fifteen minutes time had elapsed from the commencement of the row before the general and his two criminals were the only occupants of the field of action. Here bloodshed, imprisonment, trials by court-martial were happily prevented, and hostile feelings between the different corps of the army distinguished by the physical an mental energies timely exerted by one individual."

Israel Trask, 19th Century Pension Papers

"A large portion of the back settlers, living upon the Indian frontiers, are, according to the best of my information, far greater savages than the Indians themselves. It is nothing uncommon, I am told, to see hung up in their chimney corners, or nailed against the door of [their cabins, scalps. They have] employed their skins as they would have done those of a wild beast, for whatever purpose they could be applied to. An Indian is considered by them as nothing better than a destructive ravenous wild beast, without reason, without a soul, that ought to be hunted down like a wolf wherever it makes its appearance; and indeed, even amongst the bettermost sort of the inhabitants of the western country, the most illiberal [intolerant, narrow-minded] notions are entertained respecting these unfortunate people, and arguments for their banishment, or rather extirpation, are adopted, equally contrary to justice and to humanity. 'The Indian,' says they, 'who has no idea, or at least is unwilling to apply himself to agriculture, requires a thousand acres of land for the support of his family; an hundred acres will be enough for one of us and our children; why then should these heathens, who have no notion of arts and manufactures, who never have made any improvement in science, and have never been the inventors of any thing new or useful to the human species, be suffered to encumber the soil?' — 'The settlements making in the upper parts of Georgia, upon the fine lands of the Oconec and Okemulgee rivers, will,' says Mr. Imlay, speaking of the probable destination of the Indians of the south western territory, 'bid defiance to them in that quarter. The settlements of French Broad, aided by Holston, have nothing to fear from them: and the Cumberland is too puissant [powerful] to apprehend any danger. The Spaniards are in possession of the Floridas (how long they will remain so, must depend upon their moderation and good manners) and of the settlements at the Natchez and above, which will soon extend to the southern boundaries of Cumberland, so that they (the Indian) will be completely enveloped in a few years. Our people (alluding to those of the United States) will continue to encroach upon them on three sides, and compel them to live more domestic lives, and assimilate them to our mode of living, or cross to the western side of the Mississippi.'"

Isaac Weld, Travels Through the States of North America, 1799.

"[There were]. . . a great number of American riflemen along with the redcoats, who scattered out, took trees, and were good marks-men; therefore they found they could not accomplish their design, and were obliged to retreat. When returned from the battle to Fort DuQuesne, the Indians concluded that they would go to their hunting. The French endeavored to pursuade them to stay and try another battle. The Indians said if it was only the red-coats they had to do with, they could soon subdue them, but they could not withstand Ashalecoa, or the Great Knife, which was the name they gave the Virginians."

Colonel James Smith, An Account of the Remarkable Occurances
in the Life and Travels of Colonel James Smith, 1799.

"Thomas and Daniel Cresap (sons of Colonel Cresap) went out about three weeks since, with sixty People, dressed and painted like Indians, to kill the Women and Children in the Indian towns, and scalp them, while their Warriors are committing the like Destruction on our Frontiers."

Maryland Gazette, 1756.

"Between this place (Virginia) and the Blue Mountains the country is rough and hilly, and but very thinly inhabited. The few inhabitants, however, met with here, are uncommonly robust and tall; it is rare to see a man amongst them who is not six feet high. These people entertain a high opinion of their own superiority in point of bodily strength over the inhabitants of the low country. A similar race of men is found all along the Blue Mountains."

Isaac Weld, Travels Through the States of North America, 1799.

". . . the first settlers on the frontiers; in general they are men of a morose and savage disposition, and the very outcasts of society, who bury themselves in the woods, as if desirous to shun the face of their fellow-creatures; there they build a rude habitation, and clear perhaps three or four acres of land, just as much as they find sufficient to provide their families with corn: for the greater part of their food they depend on their rifle guns. These people, as the settlements advance, are succeeded in general by a second set of men, less savage than the first, who clear more land, and do not depend so much upon hunting as upon agriculture for their subsistence. A third set succeed these in turn, who build good houses, and bring the land into a more improved state. The first settlers, as soon as they have disposed of their miserable dwellings to advantage, immediately penetrate farther back into the woods, in order to gain a place of abode, suited to their rude mode of life. These are the lawless people who encroach, as I have before mentioned, on the Indian territory, and are the occasion of the bitter animosities between the whites and the Indians. The second settlers, likewise, when displaced, seek for similar places to what those that they have left were when they first took them. I found, as I proceeded through this part of the country, that there was scarcely a man who had not changed his place of abode seven or eight different times."

Isaac Weld, Travels Through the States of North America, 1799.

"Come and help me fight the King's regular Troops . . . You know they stand all along close together, rank and file, and my men fight as Indians do."

Colonel Ethan Allen, An Appeal to the Iroquois Confederacy, 1775.

"This distinguished race of men are more savage than the Indians, and posses every one of their vices, but not one of their virtues. I have known one of these fellows [to] travel two hundred miles through the woods never keeping any road or path, guided by the sun by day and the stars by night, to kill a particular person belonging to the opposite party. He would shoot him before his own door and ride away to boast of what he had done on his return."

Colonel George Hanger, To All Sportsmen and
Particularly to Farmers and Gamekeepers, 1814.

The earliest settlers of Kentucky were described as ". . . a set of scoundrels who scarcely believe in God or fear a devil . . ."

Richard Henderson, of the Transylvania Company, 1775.

"Of all useless sets that ever incumbered an Army, surely the boasted Rifle-men are certainly the most so. To be sure, there never was a more mutinous and undisciplined set of villians that bred disturbance in any camp."

Benjamin Thompson, (later Count Rumford) Boston, 1775,
who later became a professed Loyalist.

"They conduct themselves with a barbarity worthy of their savage neighbors. The ferocious practice of stage-boxing in England, is urbanity, compared with the Virginian mode of fighting. In their combats, unless specially precluded, they are admitted (to use their own terms), 'to bite, b-ll-ck, and goudge,' which operations, when the first onset with fists is over, consists in fastening on the nose or ears of their adversaries, seizing him by the genitals, and dexterously scooping out an eye; on which account it is no uncommon circumstance to meet men in the prime of youth, deprived of one of those organs."

Marquis de Chastellux, <u>Travels in North America in the Years 1780, 1781, 1782 and 1787, 1827</u>.

"Of all the uncouth human beings I met with in America, these people from the western country were the most so; their curiosity was boundless . . ."

Isaac Weld, <u>Travels Through the States of North America</u>, 1799.

"We may learn of the Indians what is useful and laudable, and at the same time lay aside their barbarous proceedings. This much to be lamented that some of our frontier rifle-men are prone to imitate them in their inhumanity."

James Smith, <u>An Account of the Remarkable Occurances in the Life and Travels of Colonel James Smith</u>, 1799.

"They are such a boastful, bragging set of people, and think none are men or can fight but themselves."

<u>A Virginian's Description of Riflemen</u>, ca. 1780.

CHAPTER 6

THE RIFLEMAN'S CLOTHING

Moccasins

On the frontier, shoes were almost nonexistant, but moccasins, which were more practical in many ways, were almost universally worn by both men and women. Their great disadvantage was that they wore out quickly. Often, a woodsman would carry several old pieces of moccasins for patching the soles of new pairs. They offered little protection to the feet and were described by one contemporary as being "a decent way of going barefoot."

Simple Center Seam Style

Pucker detail:

Joe

3/8"

1/8" apart

Each side is pinched then sewn together. Process is repeated on other side with second thread.

Oneida Style

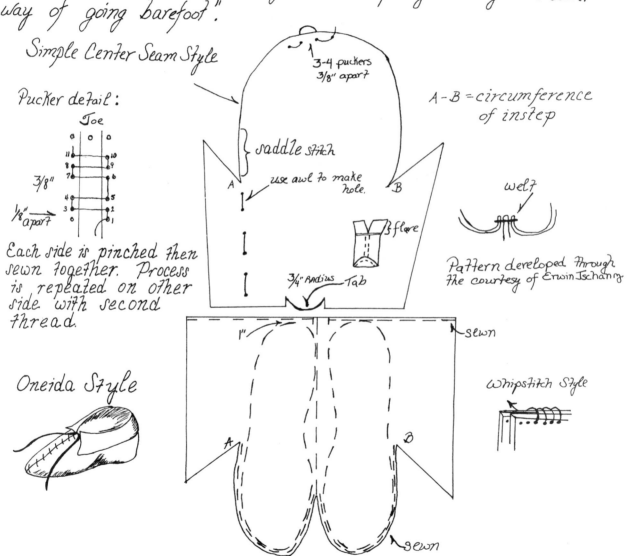

3-4 puckers 3/8" apart

A-B = circumference of instep

saddle stitch

A   use awl to make hole.   B

3 flare

3/4" Radius   Tab

1"

A   B

sewn

sewn

welt

Pattern developed through the courtesy of Erwin Tschanz.

Whipstitch Style

Shoepacks

An interesting specimen found within the walls of an upstate New York house (circa 1834), this shoepack seems to be of traditional 18th century style. The fact that it has a separate sole and the leather is smooth on one side, rough on the other, indicate it to have been the product of a whiteman.

This, after the Ft. Ligonier example, is only the second shoepack to come to light.

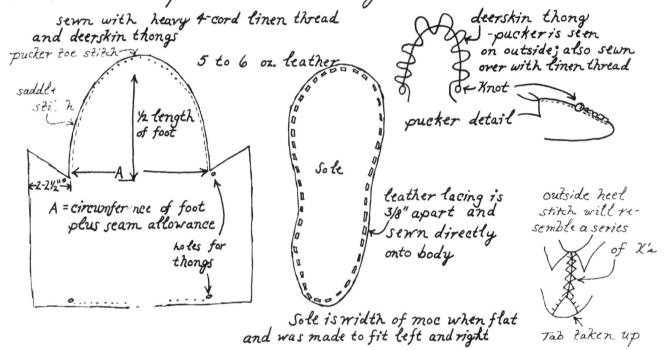

sewn with heavy 4-cord linen thread and deerskin thongs

pucker toe stitch

saddle stitch

½ length of foot

A

←2-2½"→

A = circumference of foot plus seam allowance

holes for thongs

5 to 6 oz. leather

Sole

Sole is width of moc when flat and was made to fit left and right

leather lacing is 3/8" apart and sewn directly onto body

deerskin thong -pucker is seen on outside; also sewn over with linen thread

Knot

pucker detail

outside heel stitch will resemble a series of X's

Tab taken up

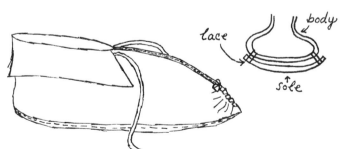

lace

body

sole

Source:
A private collection; and from a pattern developed by Erwin Tschanz.

RL

Moccasin/Shoepack

A famous, pre-Revolutionary War "moccasin" (actually more of a shoepack) found at Fort Ligonier, Penna., is illustrated here. It is made of deerskin and laced with leather thongs. Past publications have shown the leather stitching of the sole to not go all the way through, thus protecting it from wear. However, recent investigation indicates that the stitching did, indeed, penetrate the entire thickness of the sole.

This artifact is important not only because it is the earliest datable shoepack, but because it is the simple, plain style of footwear the average white settler would have worn.

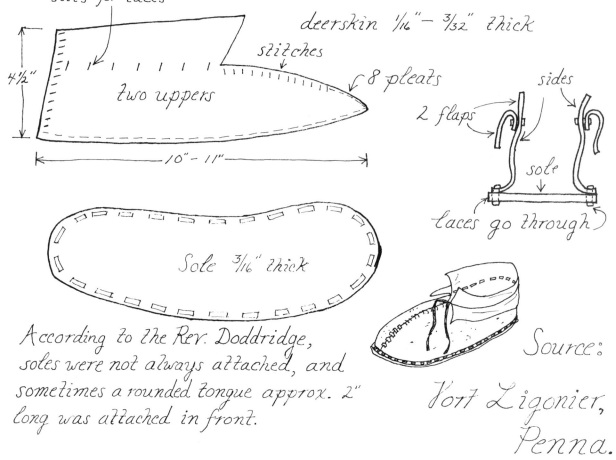

slits for laces

deerskin 1/16" - 3/32" thick

4½"

two uppers

stitches

8 pleats

10" - 11"

2 flaps

sides

sole

laces go through

Sole 3/16" thick

According to the Rev. Doddridge, soles were not always attached, and sometimes a rounded tongue approx. 2" long was attached in front.

Source:

Fort Ligonier, Penna.

92

Leggings and Garters

Leggings were often made of tanned elk or deerskin and sometimes of blue, red or green wool.

Leggings were favored by many woodsmen as they were easy to make and helped protect the leg in the forests from underbrush. Sometimes, they were worn with the Indian breechclout as some of George Rogers Clark's men did in the Illinois Country in 1778-1779, but normally the riflemen preferred their legs to be well covered and protected from brush, ticks, and insects and wore their leggings with breeches or trousers.

The leggings were often worn with one or two flaps; but sometimes without any at all; and only occasionally were they fringed (a 1" or 2" fringe). They seem to have resembled the military leggings, or full gaiters, as they fit close to the shape of the leg and usually came only half way up the thigh; occasionally they reached to the hips. Often beaded, they could be trimmed with ribbons and moose hair bristles. Most contemporary evidence indicates they were worn tucked inside the moccasins. The moccasin flaps could then be turned up for maximum protection.

Garters could be made of almost any material but most often of woven wool and decorated with the usual white trade beads.

Leggings and Garters

There are two basic styles of 18th century leggings, based on contemporary paintings, drawings and descriptions.

1. This style was more common and came about half way up the thigh.

Thong for attaching to belt

White trade beads

dyed hair bristles

silk ribbon

Garter

Garters were often made of blue, black or red wool, occasionally of woven moose hair, with white glass beads woven in.

Beads were woven in and out with a seperate thread

2. Less commonly leggings extended to the hips.

Thong

Sometimes the garters passed through slits in the flaps.

2" - 4" wide

Sometimes leggings were made simply by wrapping the material around loosely and tied with garters. In this, garters were also necessary around the ankles.

Rev. Doddridge noted that in the latter years of the Indian wars the young men became more enamored of Indian clothing and lengthened the leggings so as to reach the upper part of the thigh. (See section entitled "Verbal Accounts") This change probably occurred in the late 1770's or 1780's.

Thong is pulled through cone and attached to edge of flap.

Tin cone

buckskin

hair dyed red

Sources:

1. Numerous contemporary paintings, notably by Benjamin West.

2. Two engravings, one by W. Nutter after J. Graham of the death of Fraser at Saratoga done around 1794 and the other by Benjamin West of Col. Bouquet in 1764.

Breeches, Trousers and Overalls

Usually made of homespun linen, linsey-woolsey or deerskin, breeches and trousers were made exactly like those worn in the east, i.e., puckered back, drop flap, tight in the leg, loose in the seat, etc. However a decorative fringe was often added to the trousers. While breeches could be worn with stockings or leggings, trousers seem to have been more popular. Deerskin breeches were extremely popular in the east and it created a need for a steady supply of hides—one of the main reasons the long hunters penetrated the mountains in the late 1760's and early 1770's. Overalls were also worn by Continental riflemen. In 1778, Posey's riflemen requested overalls along with hunting shirts and shoes.

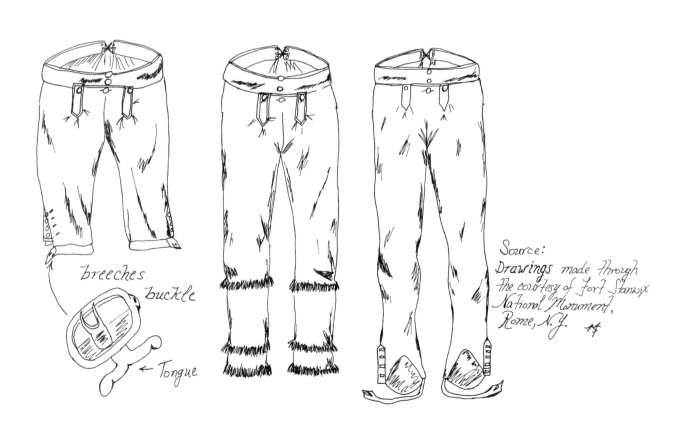

breeches

buckle

← Tongue

Source:
Drawings made through the courtesy of Fort Stanwix National Monument, Rome, N.Y.

Breechclouts

Sometimes breechclouts were preferred by frontier riflemen to the more civilized trousers. Easy to make and comfortable they were usually worn with leggings, although it is said that on occasion Long Hunters were known to be clad only in breechclouts and hunting shirts. They were most often made of a light wool broadcloth as was traded to Indians and they were usually a blue, red, or green color. Many of the Indians beaded or quilted theirs in exquisite detail and the Rev. Doddridge noted that some whites embroidered theirs after the Indian fashion.

Contemporary accounts indicate most were about 8"-9" wide.

Unlike the Plains style, breechclouts of woodland Indians were generally short, hanging perhaps a foot below the belt.

silk ribbon tapers off →

Iroquois style beadwork →

The so-called "apron" style of breechclout does not seem to be in evidence during the 18th century.

Sources: Traditional style of breechclout pictured in "League of the Ho-De-No-Sau-Nee, or Iroquois," by Lewis H. Morgan, 1851; also contemporary paintings and descriptions.

Belt Buckles

Belts were used both to keep the wrap-around hunting shirts closed and to hang the axe and long knife on. Sometimes leather thongs would suffice and other times wool sashes dyed a variety of colors, would be used. According to Rev. Doddridge, belts were tied or buckled in the back so that it could not catch on any object in the woods.

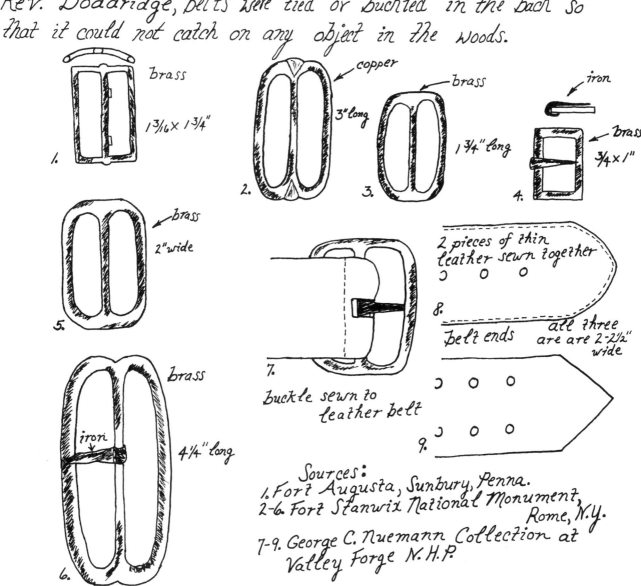

1. brass 1³⁄₁₆ × 1³⁄₄"

2. copper 3" long

3. brass 1³⁄₄" long

4. iron brass ³⁄₄ × 1"

5. brass 2" wide

6. brass iron 4¹⁄₄" long

7. buckle sewn to leather belt

8. 2 pieces of thin leather sewn together

belt ends all three are are 2-2½" wide

9.

Sources:
1. Fort Augusta, Sunbury, Penna.
2-6. Fort Stanwix National Monument, Rome, N.Y.
7-9. George C. Nuemann Collection at Valley Forge N.H.P.

Common Shirt

Men on the frontier wore the same type of shirt as the eastern people, although many favored a colorful blue and white or red and white checked shirt. The most common, however, was the usual bleached white shirt.

A rifle officer would prefer one with ruffles and they were usually made of a fine homespun linen.

Heavier shirts called frocks, often used by farmers, were basically the same style as the common shirt but made of a more coarse linen. They were sometimes dyed brown, sage green or indigo blue. A checked blue and white gingham was also used.

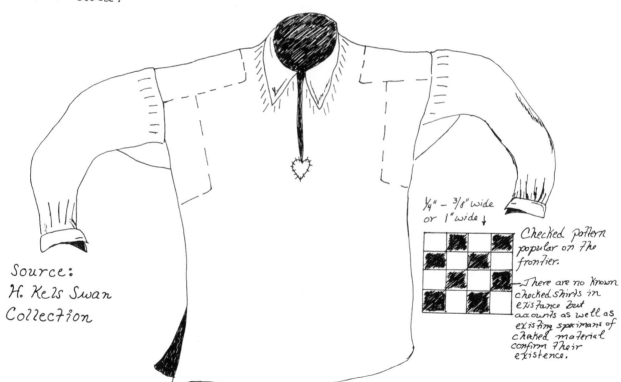

Source:
H. Kels Swan
Collection

¼" – 3/8" wide
or 1" wide ↓

Checked pattern popular on the frontier.

There are no known checked shirts in existance but accounts as well as existing specimens of checked material confirm their existence.

98

Common Shirt pattern

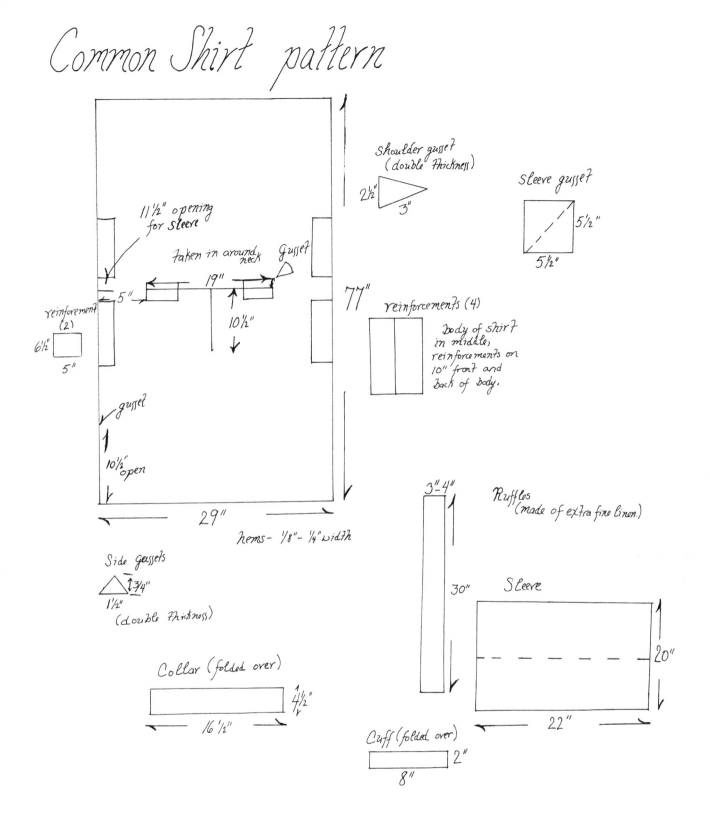

11½" opening for sleeve

Taken in around neck

Gusset

19"

5"

10½"

reinforcement (2)

6½"

5"

gusset

10½" open

29"

77"

hems - ⅛" - ¼" width

Shoulder gusset (double thickness)

2½"

3"

Sleeve gusset

5½"

5½"

reinforcements (4)

Body of shirt in middle, reinforcements on 10" front and Back of body.

Side gussets

¾"

1½"

(double thickness)

Collar (folded over)

4½"

16½"

Cuff (folded over)

2"

8"

3" 4"

30"

Ruffles (made of extra fine linen.)

Sleeve

20"

22"

Hunting Shirts

Also called "rifle shirts" or "rifle frocks", these were universally worn by the backwoodsmen from the mid-1700's until the second quarter of the 1800's after which they went gradually out of style. They were usually made of linen or linsey woolsey (only occasionally of deerskin as it got "cold and uncomfortable" in wet weather and required several days for drying) and was a highly practical garment. It retained warmth in cool weather and was comfortable in hot weather and could be easily washed in any stream or pond. Cheap and simple to make, they found favor with General Washington himself, who at one time ordered 10,000 of them to be made for the Continental Army. It was quickly adopted by the regular troops and virtually became the fatigue or battle dress of the American soldiers during the Revolutionary War.

Each hunting shirt was similar and cut along the same lines but, like the rifle, each was a bit different and reflected the owner's particular tastes. Usually, but not always, one or two capes were attached for added protection from the elements. One cape with a double row of fringe was common. A collar was usually attached to the body of the shirt and they could also have regular or puckered sleeves.

Hunting Shirts (continued)

Either pullover or wraparound, the hunting shirt was totally utilitarian. One militia unit, the Culpeper County Riflemen from Virginia had the emblem "Liberty or Death" sewn in large letters on to the front of their hunting shirts. They were dyed a variety of colors with white, brown and grey being the most common and often the fringe would be dyed a contrasting shade.

The amount of fringe was up to the wearer's particular fancy unless military orders were in effect regarding how much there should be and where it should be placed.

The average rifle frock would probably have fringe at the bottom, one or two rows around the cape and one row around each cuff. When worn with trousers the hunting shirt was not only made of the same material but was generally the same color.

Hunting Shirt (Newburgh) 1776

Made of fine, natural color linen.
This shirt was worn by Abraham Duryea, a militiaman,
during the battle of Long Island (or Brooklyn) in August, 1776.

Source:
Washington Headquarters Museum
Newburgh, N.Y., Palisades
Interstate Park Commission

Newburgh Hunting Shirt

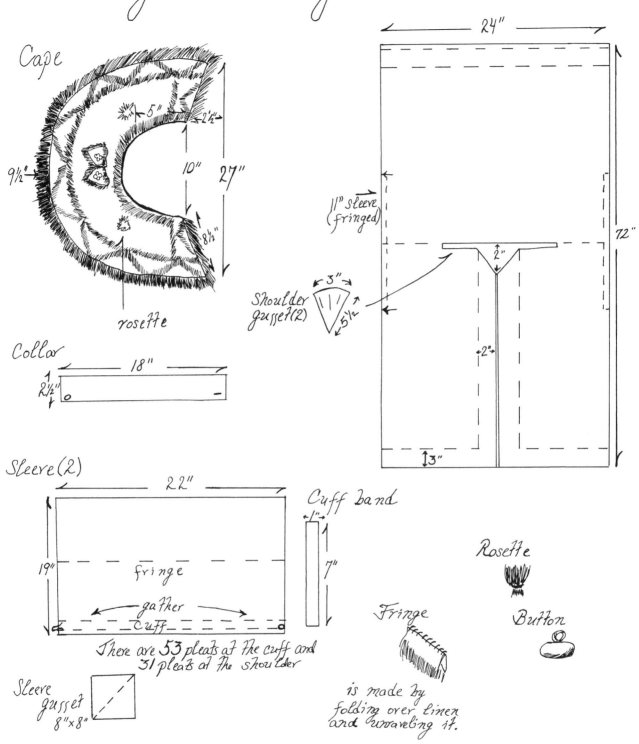

Cape

5"

2½"

9½"

10"   27"

8½"

rosette

Collar

18"

2½"

o   —

Sleeve (2)

22"

19"   fringe

gather

cuff

There are 53 pleats at the cuff and
31 pleats at the shoulder

Sleeve
gusset
8" × 8"

24"

11" sleeve
(fringed)

2"

Shoulder
gusset (2)   3"

5½"

2"

3"

72"

Cuff band

1"

7"

Rosette

Fringe

Button

is made by
folding over linen
and unraveling it.

Buckskin Hunting Shirt, 1786-1810

This particular shirt is made of deerskin with fringe at most seams and was worn by George Washington's dentist, Jean Pierre LaMayeur.

The cut is very similar to the Newburgh hunting shirt, except for the straight sleeves, the wool cuffs, and collar which could be turned up, and the attached belt.

Source:
Valentine Museum
Richmond, Virginia

This beautiful and rare hunting shirt has silk embroidery of pink, green, red and brown colors with a black velvet collar trim and cuff. The front is lined with brown cambric material, but originally the whole coat probably was so lined.

Buckskin Hunting Shirt (cont'd.)

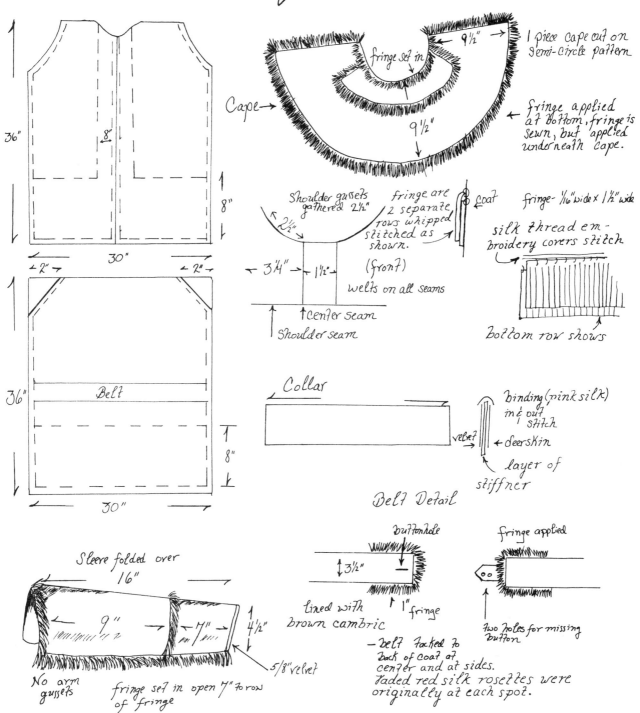

36"

8"

8"

30"

2" 2"

36"

Belt

8"

30"

1 piece cape cut on semi-circle pattern

fringe set in

9½"

9½"

Cape →

fringe applied at bottom, fringe is sewn, but applied underneath cape.

Shoulder gussets gathered 2½"

fringe are 2 separate rows whipped stitched as shown.

Coat

2½"

(front)

3¼" 1½"

welts on all seams

center seam

shoulder seam

fringe- 1/16" wide x 1½" wide

silk thread embroidery covers stitch

bottom row shows

Collar

binding (pink silk) in & out stitch

velvet → ← deerskin

layer of stiffner

Belt Detail

buttonhole

3½"

lined with brown cambric

1" fringe

fringe applied

two holes for missing button

- Belt tacked to back of coat at center and at sides. Faded red silk rosettes were originally at each spot.

Sleeve folded over 16"

9"

7"

4½"

5/8" velvet

No arm gussets

fringe set in open 7" for row of fringe

Linsey-Woolsey Hunting Shirt

This garment is similar yet different from the other known examples. The materials were woven with the intent to make the hunting shirt and the pattern is like that of other shirts of the period. As many contemporary accounts mention trousers made of the same material and color as the hunting shirt it is possible material for both was woven at the same time.

The weft is a cranberry colored wool while the warp is a natural color, creating a contrasting reddish fringe. The material is heavier than the Newburgh hunting shirt of linen, but the wool long ago lost its knap.

Said to have been worn by the Rev. Michael Crow or one of his two brothers on the Pennsylvania frontier during the Revolutionary War, this finely made speciman presents perhaps the most typical example of a hunting shirt yet found.

RL

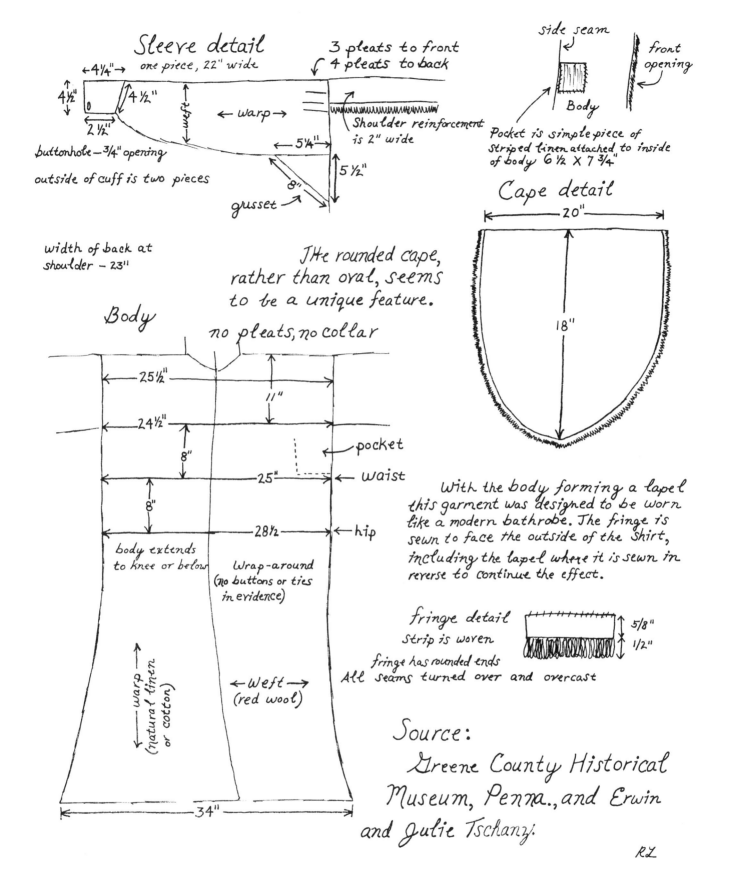

Sleeve detail
one piece, 22" wide

← 4¼" →

↕ 4½"

0   4 ½"

2 ½"

buttonhole - ¾" opening

outside of cuff is two pieces

3 pleats to front
4 pleats to back

weft

← warp →

← 5¼" →

Shoulder reinforcement
is 2" wide

5 ½"

8"

gusset ←

side seam

front opening

Body

Pocket is simple piece of
striped linen attached to inside
of body 6 ½ X 7 ¾"

width of back at
shoulder - 23"

The rounded cape,
rather than oval, seems
to be a unique feature.

no pleats, no collar

Cape detail

← 20" →

18"

Body

← 25½" →

11"

← 24½" →

8"

25"

← pocket

← waist

8"

← 28½ →

← hip

body extends
to knee or below

Wrap-around
(no buttons or ties
in evidence)

warp
(natural linen
or cotton)

← Weft →
(red wool)

34"

With the body forming a lapel
this garment was designed to be worn
like a modern bathrobe. The fringe is
sewn to face the outside of the shirt,
including the lapel where it is sewn in
reverse to continue the effect.

fringe detail
Strip is woven

5/8"
1/2"

fringe has rounded ends
All seams turned over and overcast

Source:
Greene County Historical
Museum, Penna., and Erwin
and Julie Tschanz.

RL

Northern Style Hunting Shirt, 1790-1820

This deerskin coat was made by the Iroquois Indians and presented to William Constable, Jr., one of the leading settlers of northern New York. There are several existing coats, which, made by tribes in Canada and dating to the 18th century, are very similar to this one.

It was long supposed that this was a style peculiar to that region but this specimen indicates a more southerly usage.

This style is known from collections and descriptions to have been in use before the mid-1700's. It is a pattern that could have been worn by white traders or frontiersmen of the New York or New England area.

Through Indians and traders this style of coat drifted west through Canada and was worn by the 19th century on the northern plains. The cut is remarkably similar to those shown in paintings of the mountain men of the 1800's, who may have copied the style.

An existing coat, closely related in style, was worn by Auguste Chouteau, a Rocky Mountain fur trader of the 1820's and 30's, whose base of operations was St. Louis, Missouri.

Source:
Constable Hall, Constableville, N.Y.

Northern Style Hunting Shirt (cont'd.)

William Constable, the reputed owner of the coat, died in 1804.

As no buttons or ties can be found, it was evidently a wrap-around style.

Made of brain-tanned leather, and smoked to a brownish hue.

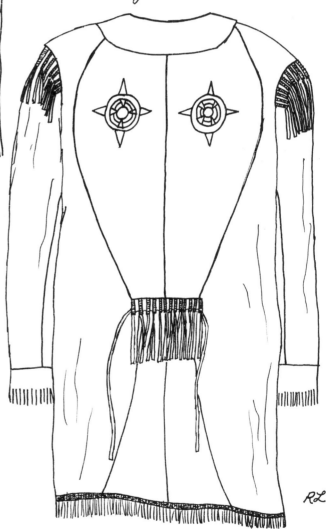

RL

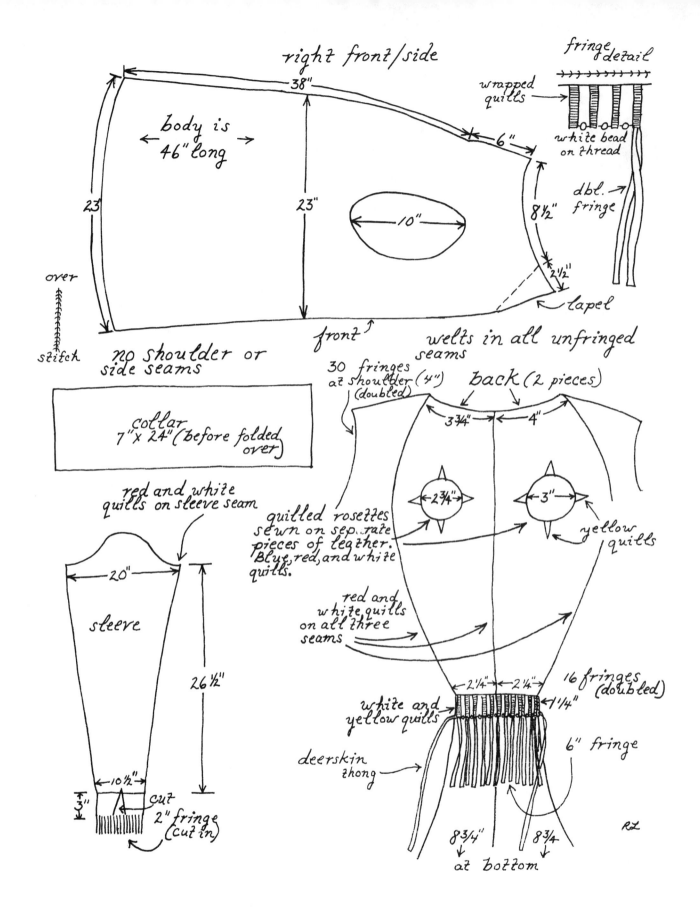

right front/side

38"

body is
46" long

23

23"

10"

over

stitch

no shoulder or
side seams

collar
7" x 24" (before folded
over)

red and white
quills on sleeve seam

sleeve

20"

26½"

10½"

3"

cut
2" fringe
(cut in)

fringe detail

wrapped
quills

white bead
on thread

dbl.
fringe

6"

8½"

2½"

lapel

welts in all unfringed
seams

30 fringes
at shoulder (4")
(doubled)

back (2 pieces)

3¾"   4"

2¾"   3"

yellow
quills

quilled rosettes
sewn on separate
pieces of leather.
Blue, red, and white
quills.

red and
white quills
on all three
seams

2¼"   2¼"

16 fringes
(doubled)

1¼"

white and
yellow quills

deerskin
thong

6" fringe

8¾"   8¾"

at bottom

RL

110

Pullover Hunting Shirt

An old photograph shows a homespun linen hunting shirt, and claims it to be a copy of an original. At the time of the books' publication in which the photograph was printed (1902), little was known about the dress of the riflemen or frontiersmen, yet this copy is accurate in all respects, and may well be a faithful reproduction of a more typical hunting shirt than those few still in existence.

The whereabouts of either the original or the copy is unknown.

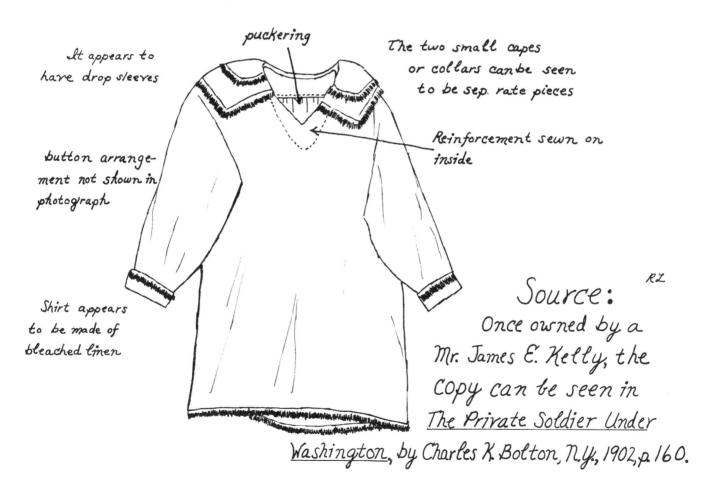

puckering

It appears to have drop sleeves

The two small capes or collars can be seen to be sep. rate pieces

Reinforcement sewn on inside

button arrange-ment not shown in photograph

Shirt appears to be made of bleached linen

Source: RZ
Once owned by a Mr. James E. Kelly, the copy can be seen in _The Private Soldier Under Washington_, by Charles K. Bolton, N.Y., 1902, p.160.

Blanket Coat (Capote)

For winter duty in Canada, British troops were issued blanket coats or "capotes" and "Canadian caps". These blanket coats were made of heavy white wool with indigo blue stripes complete with cuffs, ties, and hood. The coat bears a resemblance to a British regimental in its style and cut and is of the type that Morgan's riflemen at Quebec in 1775 would have worn. Apparently, the idea came from the winter dress of the Canadian habitants.

The are no 18ᵗʰ century blanket coats known to exist

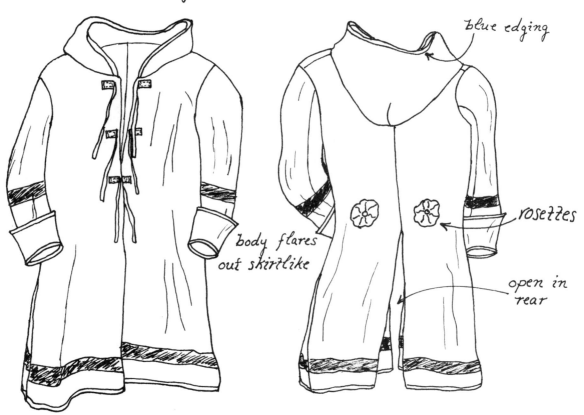

blue edging

body flares
out skirtlike

rosettes

open in
rear

Source: contemporary paintings and descriptions

Waistcoat (or Weskit)

Waistcoats, although not necessarily a part of the rifleman's dress, were worn by officers and frontier farmers. They were made of linen or fine wool twill. A buff color was favored by officers.

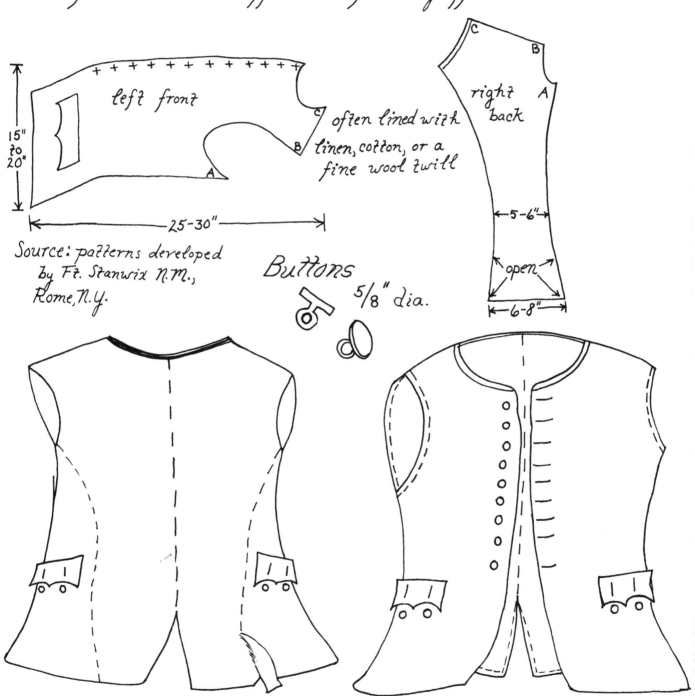

15" to 20"

left front

often lined with linen, cotton, or a fine wool twill

25-30"

Source: patterns developed by Ft. Stanwix N.M., Rome, N.Y.

Buttons

5/8" dia.

right back

5-6"

open

6-8"

Officers Stocks

Rifle officers seem to have desired stocks the same as regular army officers.

The stocks were usually made of black, or less commonly, white material, usually linen, satin or velvet; leather was used as well. If made of cloth they were about 8" to 10" wide with an inner lining to stiffen, and gathered at the ends where they could be tied or buckled. Stocks were generally tied behind or made long and tied in front.

Neck cloths were also commonly worn especially with the common work frock.

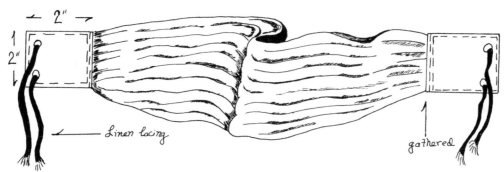

Stock made of black leather 1/10" thick.

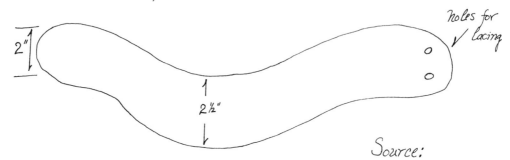

Source:
Copies at Fort Stanwix
National Monument, New York

Officer's Sash

If available, rifle officers were attired in military sashes, the same as all other officers in the army. They were made long enough to go around the waist twice, then looped over and left dangling by the left side. Meant as stretchers for wounded officers, they were made of woven silk with a wide mesh and dyed a crimson color. This particular specimen was worn by Peleg Slade, circa 1776, and is exactly like General Washington's.

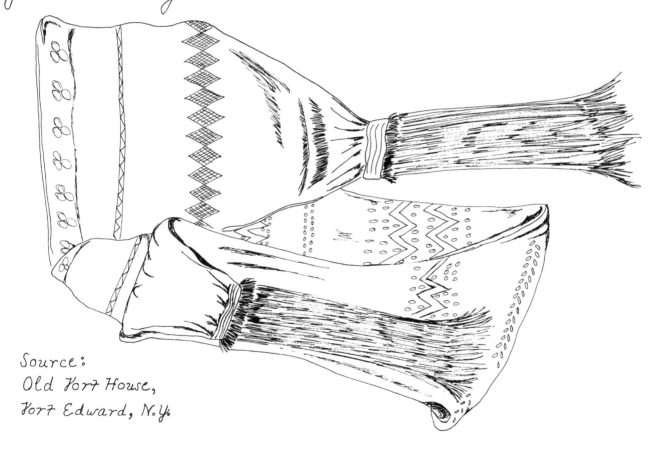

Source:
Old Fort House,
Fort Edward, N.Y.

Headgear

A "shirttail man" wore any kind of hat he desired, the most common being the low crowned, wide brimmed "flopped hat", which was generally black in color, although, some of the southern riflemen are described in white and rust colored hats, notably the "over mountain men" in Tennessee and Kentucky. These latter were more practical in a warmer climate. There was even a British regiment who were issued white flopped hats while on a southern campaign. The "round hat" was also popular. Fur hats were uncommon at this time, although the three rifle companies who went on the march to Quebec in 1775 were issued "Canadian Caps" after Montreal and all of its supplies had fallen to the Americans. Skull caps were worn by some officers and tall pointed "Congress" caps were worn by some of the men. Also, knitted caps were popular. In windy weather a simple neck cloth of fine material which was normally worn and tied around the neck, could be tied about the forehead and hair. These were about 30" by 30." When tied about the neck, it was folded crosswise and rolled into a cravat. This was tied around the neck, over or under the collar and knotted in front.

Headgear

1.
Common flapped hat was a

brimmed hat favored by farmers. Often feathers, a bucktail or green sprigs were attached. Hatbands could be a simple rope in one, two or three layers, or sometimes a snakeskin or a leather strip was used.

2.

A very common turned up "round hat" favored by many Continental riflemen as the hat would not be knocked off during drill. An original measures some 6¼" high, 10" in diameter, with a 2" double brim and is of a dull brown color.

3.

"Canadian cap" as issued to Montgomery's and Arnold's troops after Montreal and its supplies fell to the American forces in Canada. This is the type Morgan's, Hendricks', and Smiths' companies would have worn. The top is made of red or green wool, lined with fox or raccoon fur and often had a tuff of fur on top and a tail on the back. These were probably made to turn down over the ears.

4.

Skull cap of a rifleman as depicted in Barnards War in America, in 1780. These were simply regular felt hats cut down and turned up in front.

5.

"Congress" helmets as depicted in several contemporary paintings. Probably made of wool or leather. The circular device may be a circle of 13 intertwined round links "we are one".

6.

Typical knitted cap as worn by rifle troops.

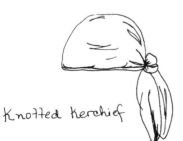

Knotted kerchief

Source:
1. description of Virginia riflemen (1775), and Arnow, Harriet, Seedtime on the Cumberland.
2. Contemporary paintings.
3. Paintings by Trumball.
4. War in America, 1780 engraving.
5. from "a real representation on the dress on American Riflemen" a Bavarian engraving.
6. Contemporary engravings and drawings.
7. Simms, Jeptha, History of Schoharie County.

CHAPTER 7

THE RIFLEMAN'S ACCOUTREMENTS

Axes

Next to his rifle, the axe was the frontiersman's most important implement. One felling axe was all most pioneers had when they invaded the wilderness to carve out a home for their families.

Belt axes were usually carried towards the back and on the left side by most riflemen. The belt axe was not properly a tomahawk, as it was substantially larger and was used mainly for camp duties such as obtaining firewood.

Tomahawks were relatively small and were primarily made for the purpose of splitting open an enemy's skull. These were usually obtained by the Indians through the fur trade, and were found light and comfortable to carry. The names 'tomahawk' and 'belt axe' were often used interchangably.

Camp axes, or three-quarter size axes, though smaller than felling axes, were large enough to do a substantial amount of the chopping around camp, and yet were still of a small enough size for convenient transportation.

Felling axes were used for dropping any size tree, and worked well for trimming off the branches. They were very handy for notching the logs to be used in a cabin, and with the aid of wedges, they were able to do a good job splitting firewood.

Axes (continued)

The Broad axe, by far the largest of the axes, was designed for hewing logs into square timbers. Although most of the structures first built in the wilderness were made of unhewn logs, in the later, more formal two storied houses the logs almost certainly were hewn.

The technique of forging together the parts of an axe:

the iron head

the completed axe head

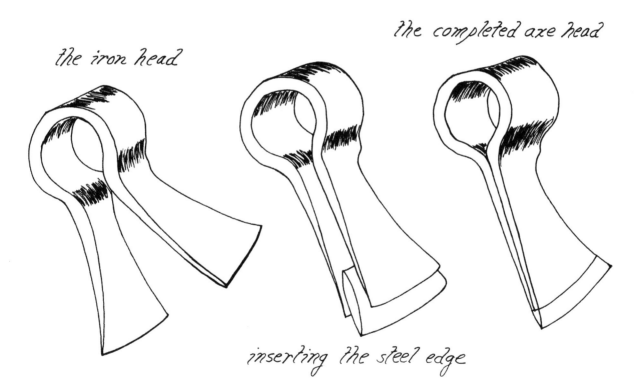

inserting the steel edge

Belt Axes

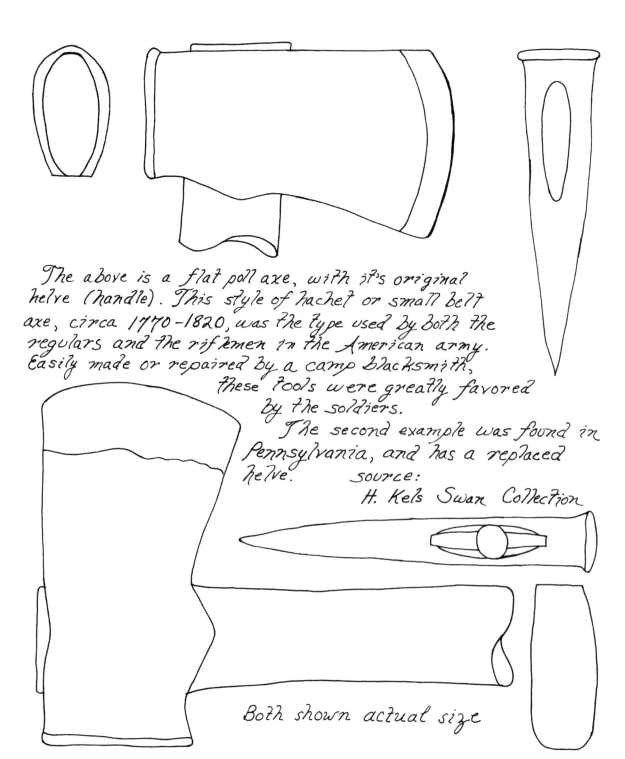

The above is a flat poll axe, with it's original helve (handle). This style of hachet or small belt axe, circa 1770-1820, was the type used by both the regulars and the riflemen in the American army. Easily made or repaired by a camp blacksmith, these tools were greatly favored by the soldiers.

The second example was found in Pennsylvania, and has a replaced helve. source:
H. Kels Swan Collection

Both shown actual size

Belt Axes (continued)

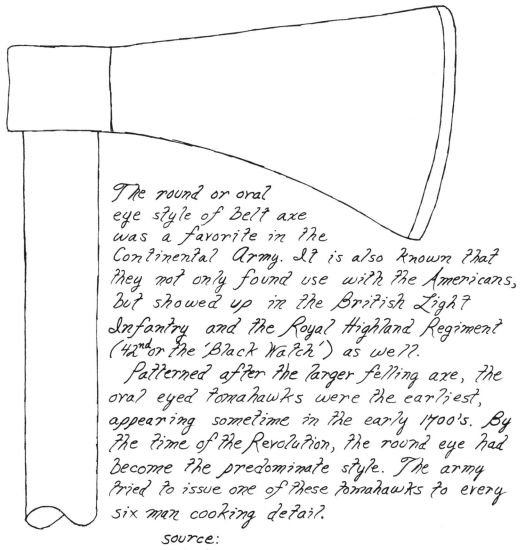

The round or oval
eye style of Belt axe
was a favorite in the
Continental Army. It is also known that
they not only found use with the Americans,
but showed up in the British Light
Infantry and the Royal Highland Regiment
(42nd or the 'Black Watch') as well.
  Patterned after the larger felling axe, the
oral eyed tomahawks were the earliest,
appearing sometime in the early 1700's. By
the time of the Revolution, the round eye had
become the predominate style. The army
tried to issue one of these tomahawks to every
six man cooking detail.
     source:
     H. Kels Swan Collection

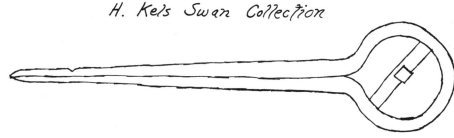

123

Belt Axes (continued)

Three typical belt axes, all with polls.
These were the type of hand weapons used
by the Indians, the frontiersmen, and
the colonial soldiers.

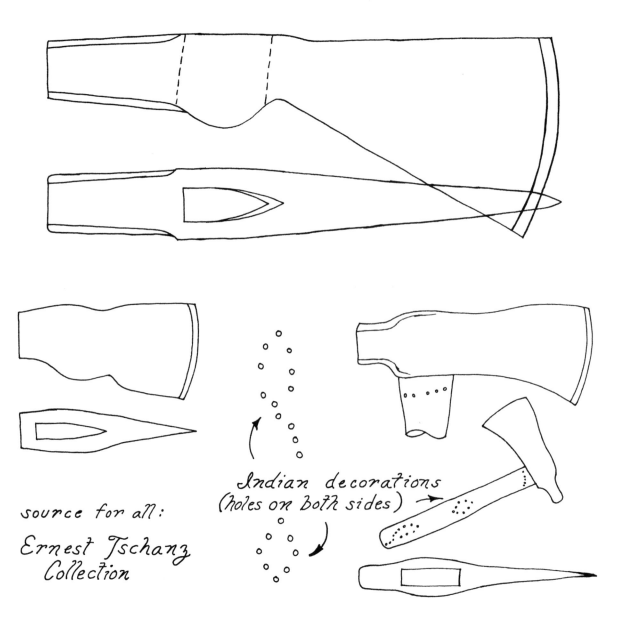

Indian decorations
(holes on both sides)

source for all:
Ernest Tschanz
Collection

Poll Axe

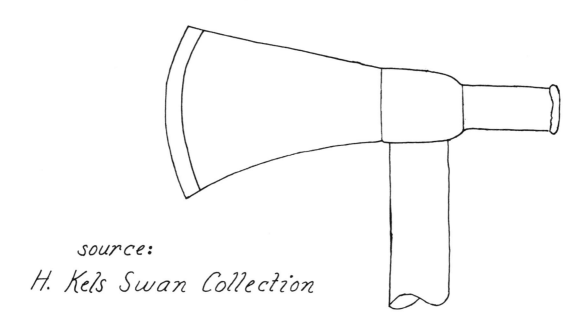

source:

H. Kels Swan Collection

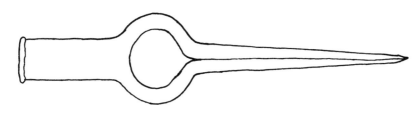

A flat hammer-poll style of belt axe or
tomahawk of the type used between 1750
and 1820 by frontier riflemen. This axe
originated in Buck's County, Pennsylvania
and was carried by a rifleman during the
Revolution in place of a bayonet. The
handle is a replacement.

Pipe Tomahawks

Pipe tomahawks were popular trade items in the fur trade.

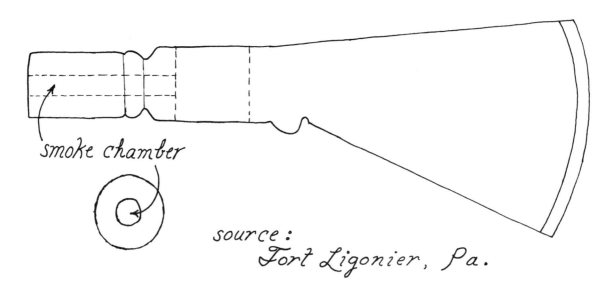

smoke chamber

source:
Fort Ligonier, Pa.

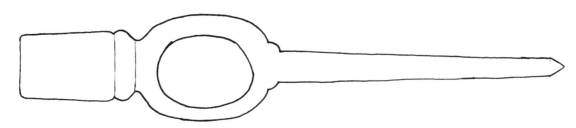

This example was found with Indian trade and presentation silver from disturbed burial sites near Waterville, Lucan County, Ohio, on the left bank of the Maumee River about fifteen miles southeast of modern Toledo.

Pipe Tomahawks (continued)

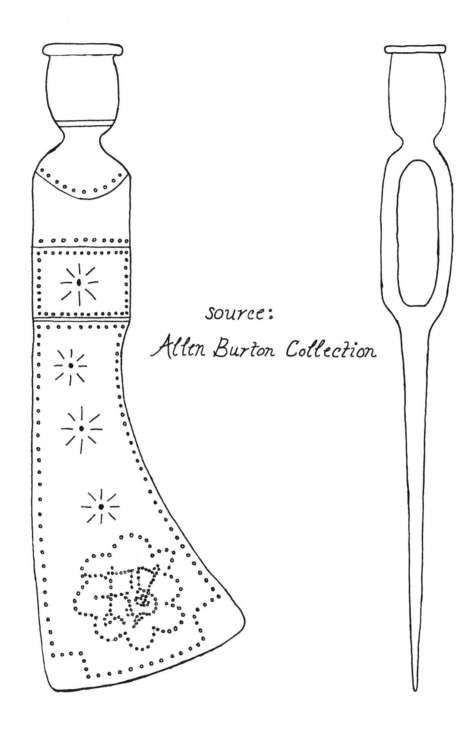

source:

Allen Burton Collection

Halberd Tomahawks

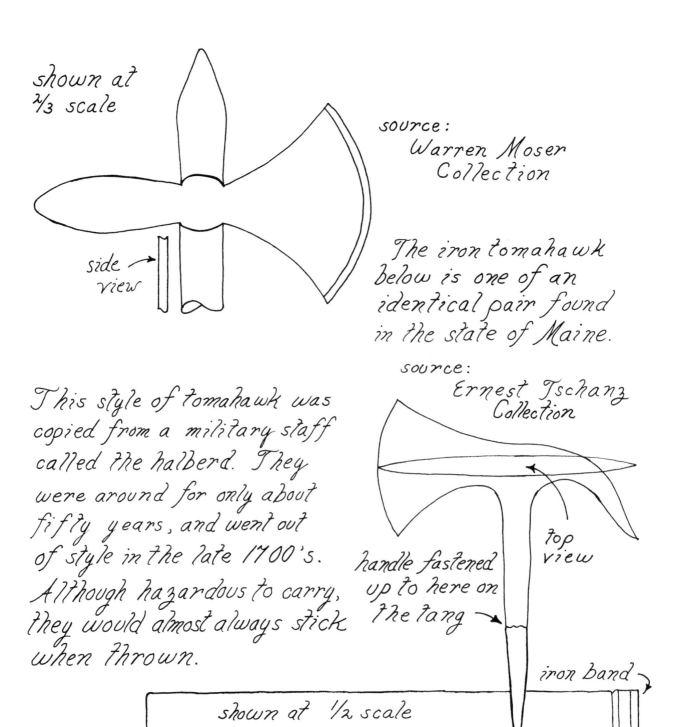

shown at ⅔ scale

side view

source:
Warren Moser
Collection

The iron tomahawk below is one of an identical pair found in the state of Maine.

source:
Ernest Tschanz
Collection

This style of tomahawk was copied from a military staff called the halberd. They were around for only about fifty years, and went out of style in the late 1700's. Although hazardous to carry, they would almost always stick when thrown.

top view

handle fastened up to here on the tang

iron band

shown at ½ scale

Spiked Tomahawks

Few spike poled axes were seen around the Revolutionary camps, for the users found that the spike was as likely to injure them as easily as the victim. The length of the spike was constantly being shortened until it entirely disappeared by the 1800's.

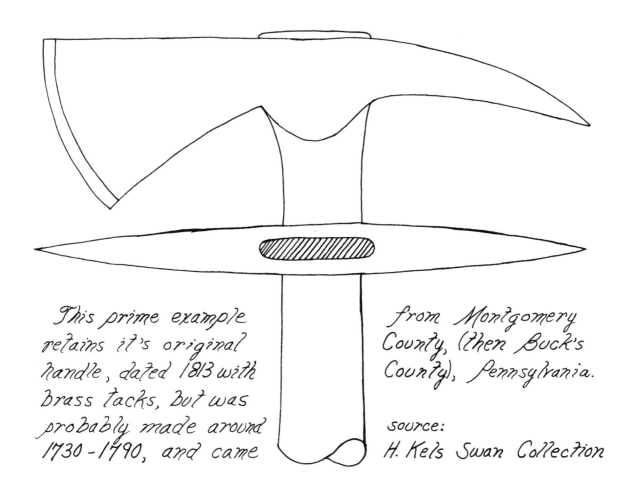

This prime example retains it's original handle, dated 1813 with brass tacks, but was probably made around 1730 - 1790, and came from Montgomery County, (then Buck's County), Pennsylvania.

source:
H. Kels Swan Collection

Spiked Tomahawks (continued)

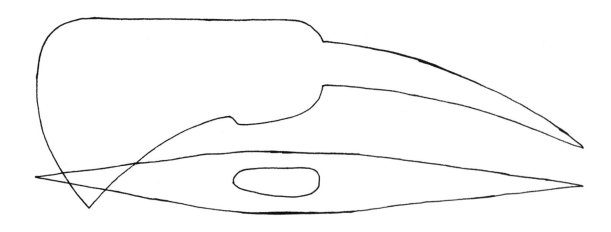

This spiked tomahawk was found at a traders
camp near Indian Castle, New York.

source:
Warren Moser Collection

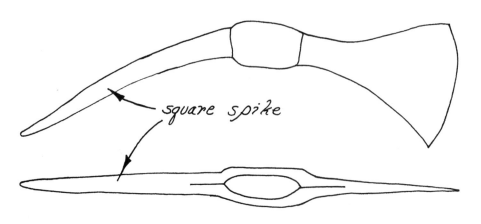

square spike

circa 1700-1800
shown at ⅔ scale

source:
Jubal Earley Collection

Camp Axes

Both of these camp axes are iron with steel edges. These axe heads would have been mounted on straight handles.

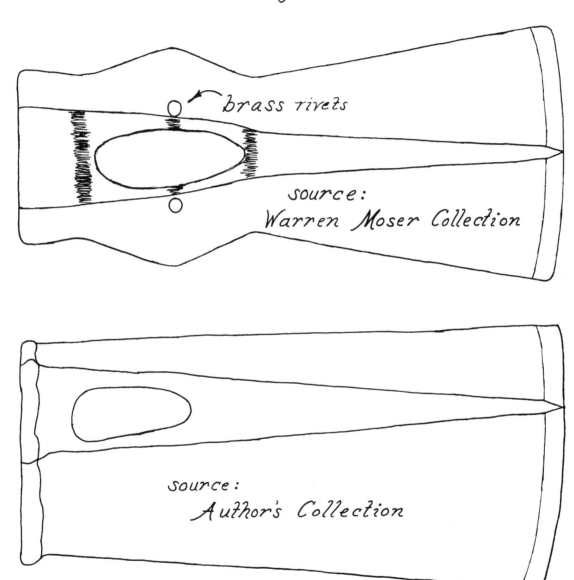

brass rivets

source:
Warren Moser Collection

source:
Author's Collection

Camp Axes (continued)

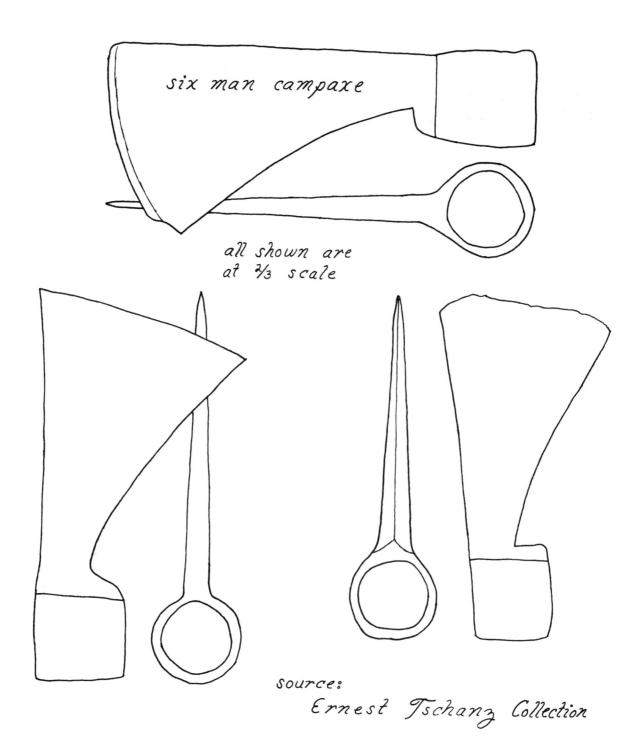

six man campaxe

all shown are
at 2/3 scale

source:
Ernest Tschanz Collection

Felling Axes

Perhaps the most important of all the axes, the felling axe was used by every pioneer family. Along with being a major tool in the construction of cabins and other buildings, the felling axe played an important everyday role, being used for such things as the making of furniture and splitting firewood.

This example is of a very early style, and probably dates from the early 1700's. It resembles the common shape of the tomahawk.

source:

Jubal Earley Collection

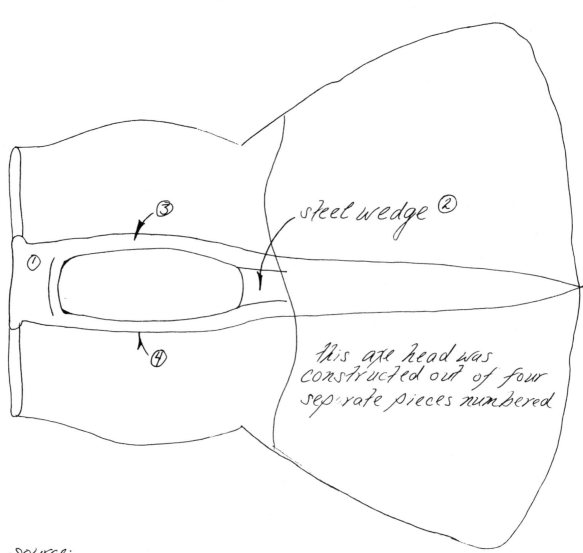

steel wedge ②

This axe head was constructed out of four separate pieces numbered

source:
Authors Collection

Knives

All backwoodsmen carried blades, commonly called "hunting", "scalping", and "long" knives. Actually the so-called "scalping knives" or "scalpers" which the British were trading to the Indians at the western forts had a relatively short blade, virtually the same as the common butcher knives.

The "long knife" or "hunting knife" that the riflemen carried was a much larger weapon, usually eight to fourteen inches long. Often these knives were either homemade or the product of a local blacksmith.

Patch knives were made in a variety of ways, and no two of these knives were ever alike. These knives were primarily used to cut patches, pieces of cloth or leather which were wrapped around the rifle ball to insure a tight fit against the rifling in the barrel of the weapon. Handles were often made of either antler, wood, or cow horn, and were attached to the three to four inch blades with a mixture of pine resin. These knives were carried in a sheath which was fastened either to the strap of the hunting pouch or directly behind the pouch itself.

overall length - 11½"

The classic long knife - stag handle, iron rivets, steel blade.

source:
Jubal Earley Collection

135

Long Knives

Though many long knives were similar, no two were exactly alike. All three of these excellent examples are home made, and they all have antler handles. Most of the weapons like these were devoid of any type of guard.

It has been said that it was knives like these that gave the name "Big Knives" to the Kentuckians.

This diagram is shown at 1/2 scale.

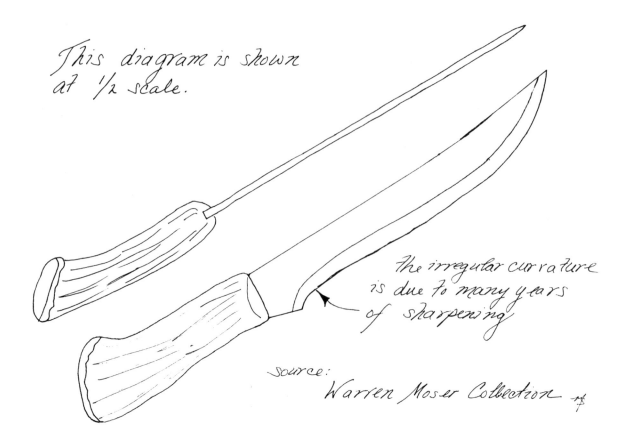

The irregular curvature is due to many years of sharpening

source:
Warren Moser Collection

Long Knives (continued)

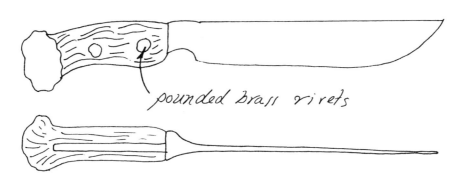

pounded brass rivets

source:

Valley Forge Historical Society

Both knives are shown at 1/3 scale

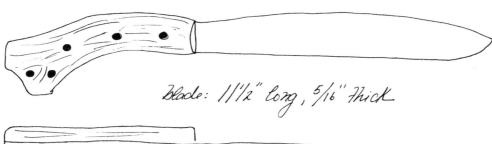

Blade: 11 1/2" long, 5/16" thick

two pieces of antler riveted to blade

With a total length of 18 3/4" and a total weight of one and one-half pounds, the knife pictured above could have been used for chopping as well as cutting.

source:

George C. Newmann Collection, Valley Forge N.H.P.

Long Knives (cont'd.)

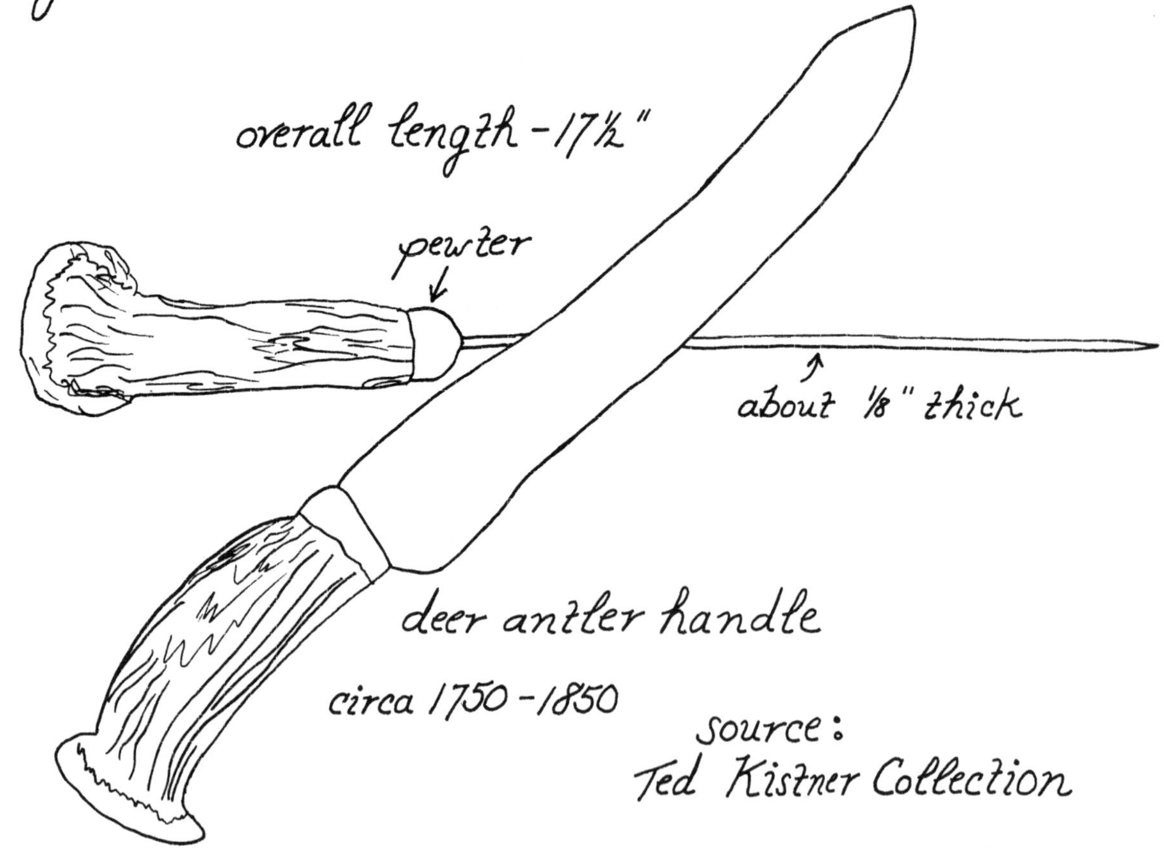

overall length – 17½"

pewter

about ⅛" thick

deer antler handle

circa 1750 – 1850

source:
Ted Kistner Collection

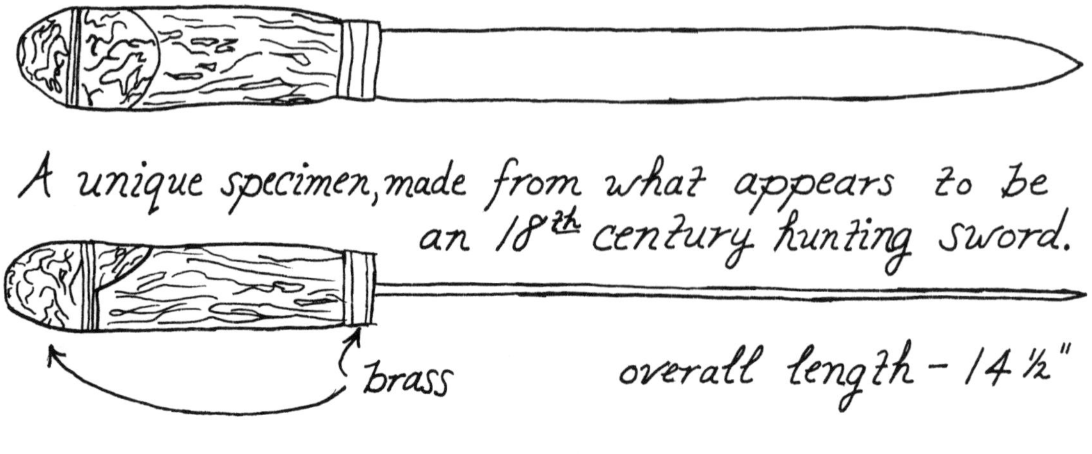

antler handle

A unique specimen, made from what appears to be an 18th century hunting sword.

brass

overall length – 14½"

source: Gil Dabkowski

RL

Long Knives (continued)

An original, hand-forged
blade that was recently
found buried in the Ohio
Valley, near the Ohio -
Kentucky border.

shown at ½ scale

source:
Glen Jackson

Scalping Knives

both are shown at 1/2 scale

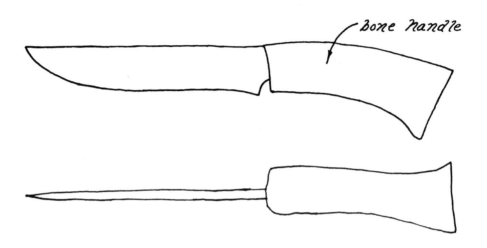

bone handle

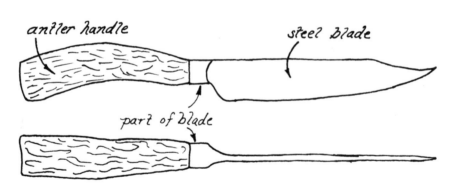

antler handle

steel blade

part of blade

source:

Allen Burton Collection

Scalping Knives (continued)

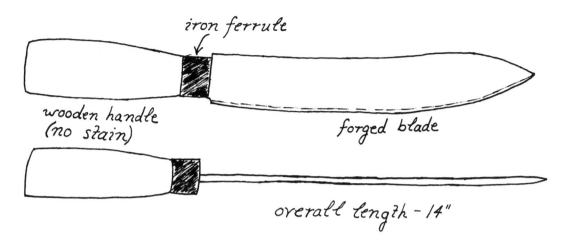

iron ferrule

wooden handle
(no stain)

forged blade

overall length – 14"

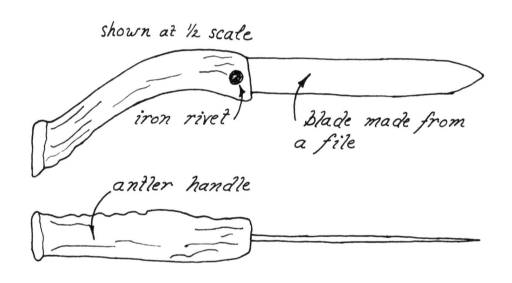

shown at ½ scale

iron rivet

blade made from
a file

antler handle

source:
top – a private collection
bottom – Jubal Earley Collection

Scalping Knives (continued)

This knife belongs with the enlisted man's hunting pouch (see hunting pouches), and is a scalping (not British issue) or hunting blade which could also have been used for cutting patches. Double-edged, it was originally carried in a belt sheath, and was later transferred to the hunting bag's strap.

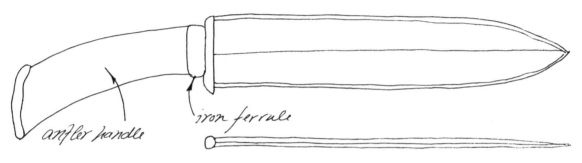

antler handle

iron ferrule

pommel detail

iron tang, peened over

Both drawings are shown ⅔ scale
source:
H. Kels Swan Collection

Black leather sheath

leather reinforce

Brass piece 1/16" thick

Although this has a piece of brass sewn on to hold it to the belt, most knife sheaths were simply thrust between the waist-belt and the body.

Scalping, Scraping Knives (continued)

This hunting, fighting or scalping knife, designed to be worn at the belt, was found in Pennsylvania, and can be dated circa 1775-1850. Made of iron, wood, and pewter, it has a six inch, hand-forged, iron blade and crudely forged brass quillons.

source:
H. Kels Swan Collection

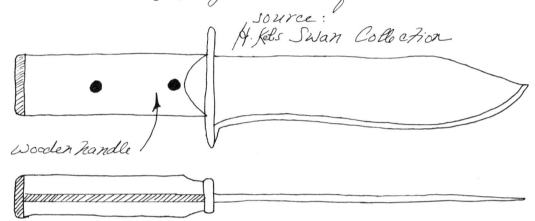

wooden handle

Both knives are shown at 2/3 scale

Bone handle

iron blade

Scraping knife of a style worn by all hunters. This one belonged to Daniel Boone. Circa 1760-1820.

source:
BlueLicks Battlefield State Park, Kentucky.

Officers' Daggers

Daggers were a favorite sidearm of many officers. Both of the following specimens were crudely fashioned by a blacksmith, and have bone or antler handles fastened to iron blades.

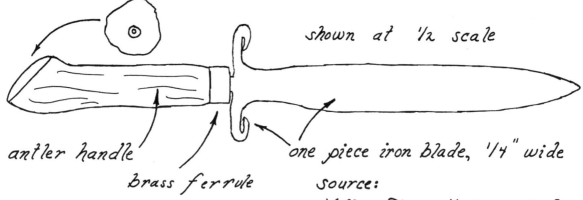

shown at ½ scale

antler handle

brass ferrule

one piece iron blade, ¼" wide

source:

Valley Forge Historical Society

This particular dagger, dated between 1760 and 1780, was found in Hatboro, Penn. Since there were no regulations governing design, daggers were made according to the owner's taste. Usually they had a doubled edged blade, six to seven inches long, and some form of a guard.

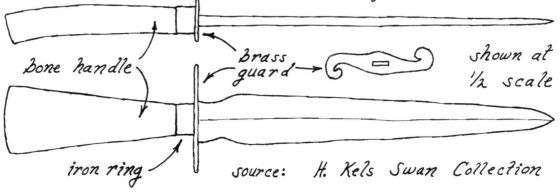

bone handle

brass guard

shown at ½ scale

iron ring

source: H. Kels Swan Collection

Patch Knives

This patch knife came from an upper New York State grave site, and is dated 1741 on the handle. It is made with a 3½" forged iron blade with a bone handle.

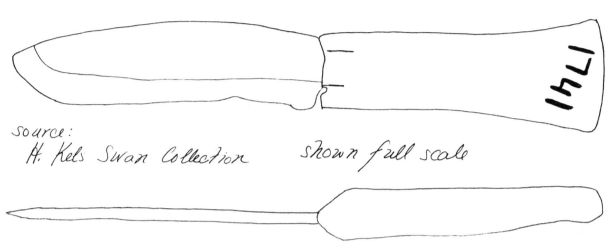

source:
H. Kels Swan Collection

shown full scale

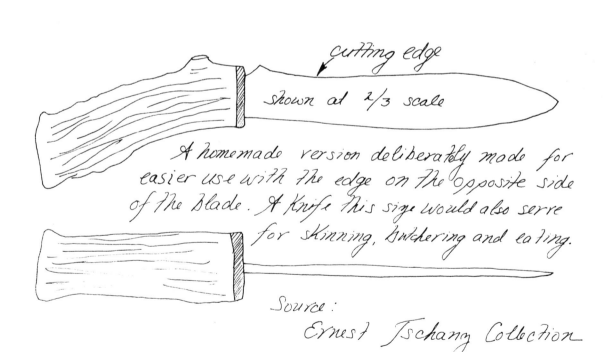

cutting edge

shown at 2/3 scale

A homemade version deliberately made for easier use with the edge on the opposite side of the blade. A knife this size would also serve for skinning, butchering and eating.

Source:
Ernest Tschanz Collection

Folding Knives

The jackknife was a common tool used by all the soldiers in the Continental Army. Some states even thought so highly of this instrument that their milita was required to carry them. Always made with a single blade, they were used for eating, whittling, artistic engraving (horn and bone) and cutting patches for the rifles and muskets. Some even came equipped with a fork for eating.

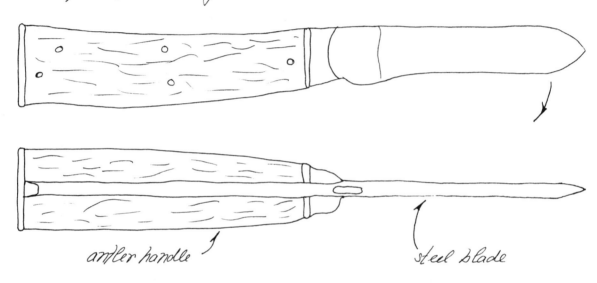

antler handle   steel blade

This specimen was used by Pennsylvania troops who were encamped at Morristown, New Jersey during the winter of 1780-81. It is typical of those used by American infantry during the Revolution.

source:
H. Kels Swan Collection

Folding Knives (continued)

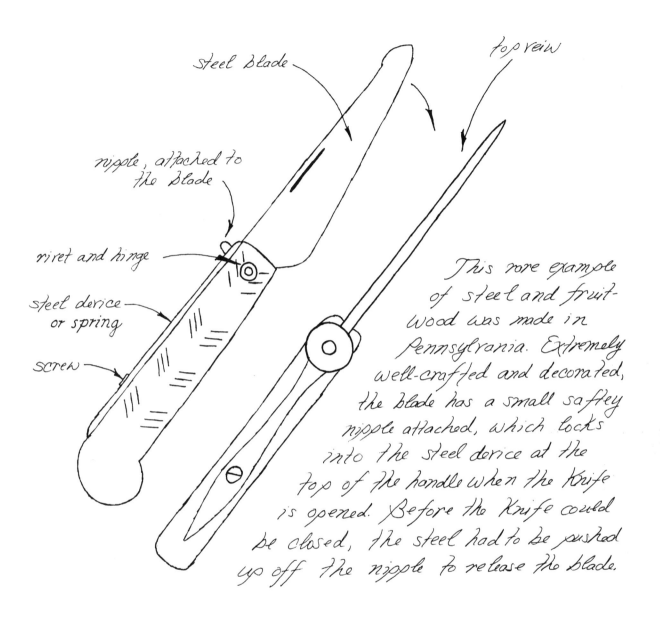

top view

steel blade

nipple, attached to
the blade

rivet and hinge

steel derice
or spring

screw

This rare example
of steel and fruit-
wood was made in
Pennsylvania. Extremely
well-crafted and decorated,
the blade has a small safety
nipple attached, which locks
into the steel derice at the
top of the handle when the knife
is opened. Before the knife could
be closed, the steel had to be pushed
up off the nipple to release the blade.

source:
H. Kels Swan Collection

Scalps and Scalping

Practiced by both whites and Indians, scalping was an accepted and common form of warfare.

There are many accounts of riflemen taking Indian scalps and on occasion even Tory and British scalps. Some authorities have stated that Col. John Butler at Fort Niagara and Col. Henry Hamilton at Detroit paid the Indians $8 bounties for the scalps of American farmers or settlers, and lesser amounts for women and children. In fact, an affidavit of William Sommer, written on July 15, 1781 and recorded in "The Public Papers of Gov. George Clinton" states that Barent Fry of Butler's Rangers and Joseph Brant, the Mohawk chieftain, offered him and his associates, "Ten Dollars for every Scalp we took". Benjamin Franklin once noted in an unproven and controversial account, an occasion in which the Iroquois attempted to present to the British several packages of scalps which totaled over 1000, of which only about 40 were from soldiers, the rest belonging to men, women and children.

It is definitely known the British presented gifts to the Indians in exchange for scalps and most frontiersmen didn't care to draw the fine line between paid bounties and rewards. Although prisoners were worth more, the Tories and Indians certainly found it more convenient to carry a scalp than to carry a captive back to the British. Evidence seems to indicate more were killed rather than captured.

Scalps and Scalping (con't.)

The following was the usual method of taking a scalp: First, the victim was tomahawked and perhaps not even killed (the border war annals are full of incidents in which victims were scalped and survived). Next, a small butcher knife or "scalper" (usually supplied by the British) was applied to the crown of the head where a small incision, circular in shape (2" or 3" in diameter), would be made. Then a foot was placed behind the victim's neck or back and one hand was placed with a firm grip on the hair. Then the scalper made a quick jerk, the head was pulled backwards, and the hair made a popping sound as it tore off. It was then stretched on a hoop, dried, often decorated and then worn on the belt or the end of a gun where it was displayed with pride.

Although a repulsive subject to more refined people and a blot on both our frontier and Indian past, scalping was nevertheless a daily occurance on the frontiers and deserves notice as a matter of fact.

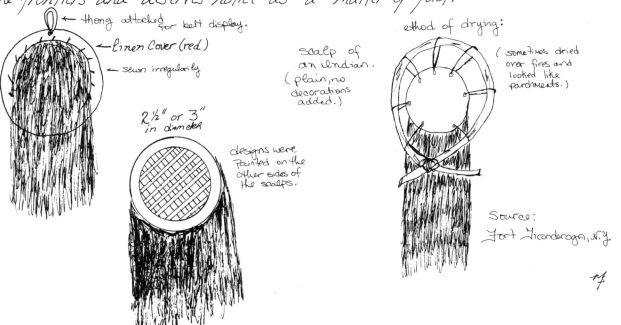

← thong attached for belt display.

← Linen Cover (red)

← sewn irregularly

Scalp of an Indian. (plain, no decorations added.)

2½" or 3" in diameter

designs were painted on the other sides of the scalps.

method of drying:

(sometimes dried over fires and looked like parchments.)

Source: Fort Ticonderoga, N.Y.

Scalps and Scalping (cont.)

Scalps, sent to the British had to be marked the right sex and age for proper payment to be given. Usually, they were packed in bundles of 90-100 scalps, and then 8 to 20 bundles were shipped together, ordinarily to the governor of Canada in Quebec. There were at least 700 scalps per shipment. The willow hoops and inside of the skin were both painted certain colors and with certain markings:

Four-inch hoop painted black ... Soldier
Four-inch hoop painted red ... Man other than soldier
Four-inch hoop painted green ... old person
Four-inch hoop painted blue ... women
Two-inch hoop painted green ... Boy
Two-inch hoop painted yellow ... Girl
Two-inch hoop painted white ... Infant
Skin painted red ... Officer
Skin painted brown ... farmer killed in house
Skin painted green ... farmer killed in field
Skin painted white ... Infant
Skin painted yellow ... Girl
Skin painted white with red tears ... Mothers
Hair braided ... Wives
Black spot in center of skin ... killed by bullet
Red hoe in center of skin ... Farmer
Black ax in center of skin ... settler
Black tomahawk in center of skin ... killed by tomahawk

Powder Horns

Powder horns and priming horns were made by trimming off both ends of a cow or ox horn. A hole would then be bored into the horn from the small, or tip end, until it reached the cavity in the horn. Next the horn itself would be scraped down to the desired thickness with a knife or file, after which a plug would be fitted into the large end, sealing the container to hold the black powder and protect it from dampness.

Sometimes these horns were scraped so thin and smooth that the level of black powder contained inside could be seen by holding them against a source of light. Many horns were carved and engraved with exquisite maps or hunting scenes. Some were done by proffesionals, and others were made by the individuals who used them.

Horns came shaped to fit either the left or right side, which side a particular horn would fit depended on which side of the animal's head it was cut from.

Powder Horns (continued)

The basic components and construction of the powder horn:

priming horns, used to carry a finer priming powder, were smaller versions of the big horns

the horns were either scraped clear, or were engraved and carved with a favorite design

a wooden plug would be inserted to seal the horn

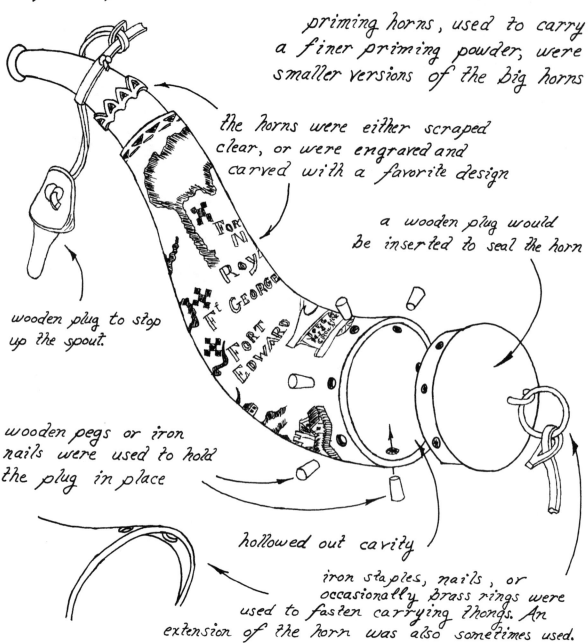

wooden plug to stop up the spout.

wooden pegs or iron nails were used to hold the plug in place

hollowed out cavity

iron staples, nails, or occasionally brass rings were used to fasten carrying thongs. An extension of the horn was also sometimes used.

Hunting Bag,

The hunting bag, or pouch, was designed to hold the rifleman's priming horn, patches, lead rifle balls, powder measures, and extra flints. This example is made of deerskin with the hair still on the outer panel. It has a "charger" or measure made from the tip of an antler, and attached to the strap is a knife that could be used for hunting and fighting as well as cutting patches. Circa 1753 to 1810, this pouch was found in a New Jersey chicken coop.

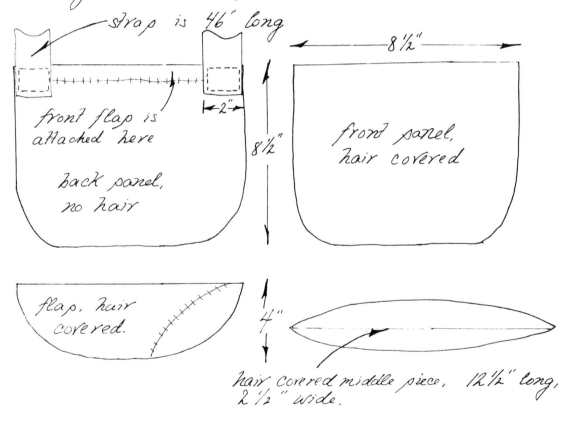

strap is 46" long

front flap is attached here

2"

back panel, no hair

8½"

8½"

front panel, hair covered

flap, hair covered.

4"

hair covered middle piece, 12½" long, 2½" wide.

Hunting Bag (continued)

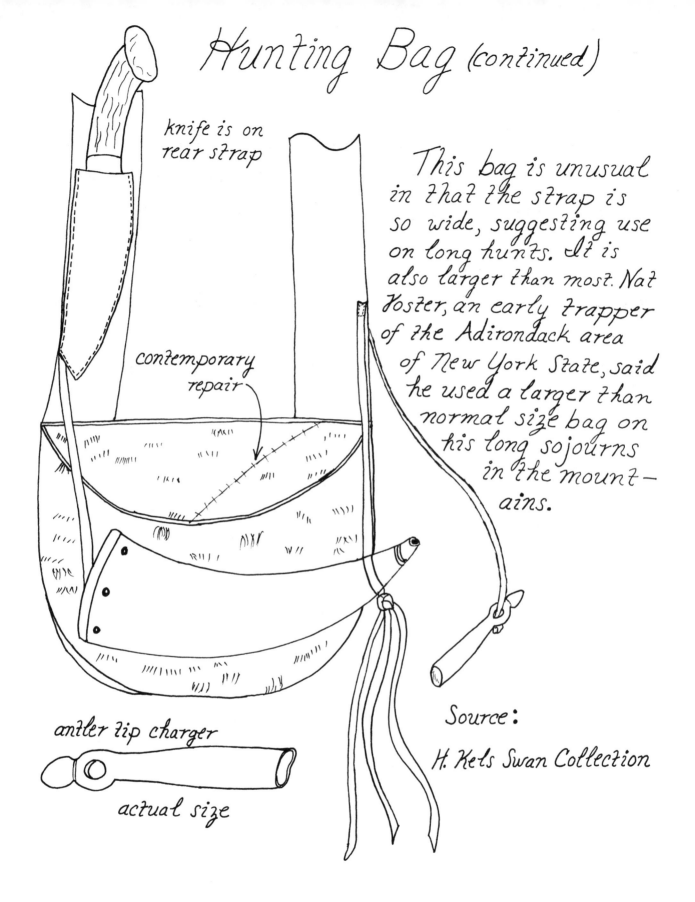

knife is on rear strap

contemporary repair

This bag is unusual in that the strap is so wide, suggesting use on long hunts. It is also larger than most. Nat Foster, an early trapper of the Adirondack area of New York State, said he used a larger than normal size bag on his long sojourns in the mountains.

Source:
H. Kels Swan Collection

antler tip charger

actual size

Hunting Pouch,

is a typical two piece pouch, hand sewn or laced, and has only one pocket.

two pieces, plus welt

thongs for horn

welt

allow ½ inch on all sides for the seams

Material is brown leather, about 3/16 of an inch thick

No ties or buttons

welt

shown at ⅔ scale

Source: King's Mountain National Military Park, S.C.

Hunting Pouch

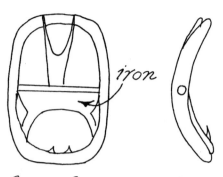

iron

brass buckle, actual size

This example was used solely for military purposes. Relatively small in size, it is light-weight and water-tight, probably the possession of an officer. Circa 1750-1800, it retains it's original brass strap buckle.

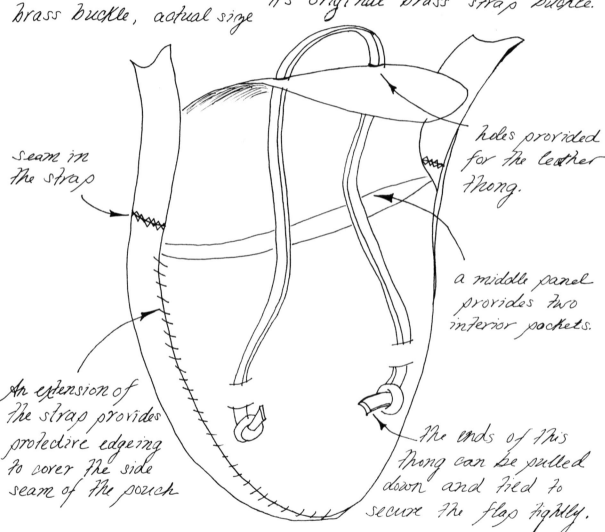

seam in the strap

holes provided for the leather thong.

a middle panel provides two interior pockets.

An extension of the strap provides protective edgeing to cover the side seam of the pouch

The ends of this thong can be pulled down and tied to secure the flap tightly.

Pouch (continued)

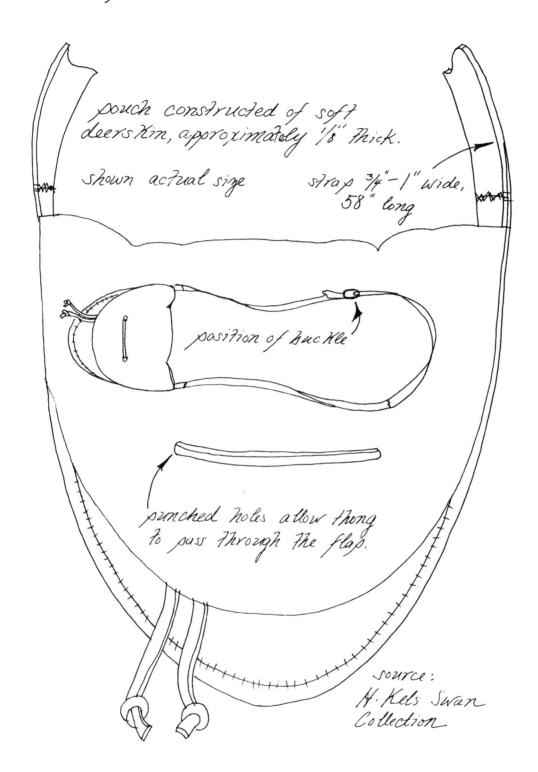

pouch constructed of soft deerskin, approximately 1/8" thick.

shown actual size   strap 3/4" - 1" wide, 58" long

position of buckle

punched holes allow thong to pass through the flap.

source:
H. Kels Swan Collection

Hunting Pouches (cont.)

drawing at 2/3 scale

A typical, one pocket pouch made of black leather, approximately 1/8" thick. This hunting pouch can be dated somewhere between 1750 and 1800.

source:
Hershey Museum of American Life, Hershey, Pennsylvania.

3/4" shoulder strap

leather binding over top, crudely attached

plain gilt brass button

Two flaps sewn together to make the pocket (aprox. 6 1/2" × 7").

sewn all around with flaxen thread, no binding on the seam of the pocket.

Hunting Pouches (cont'd.)

A well-made example of a single pocket hunting bag. It was probably a saddlebag turned into a pouch.

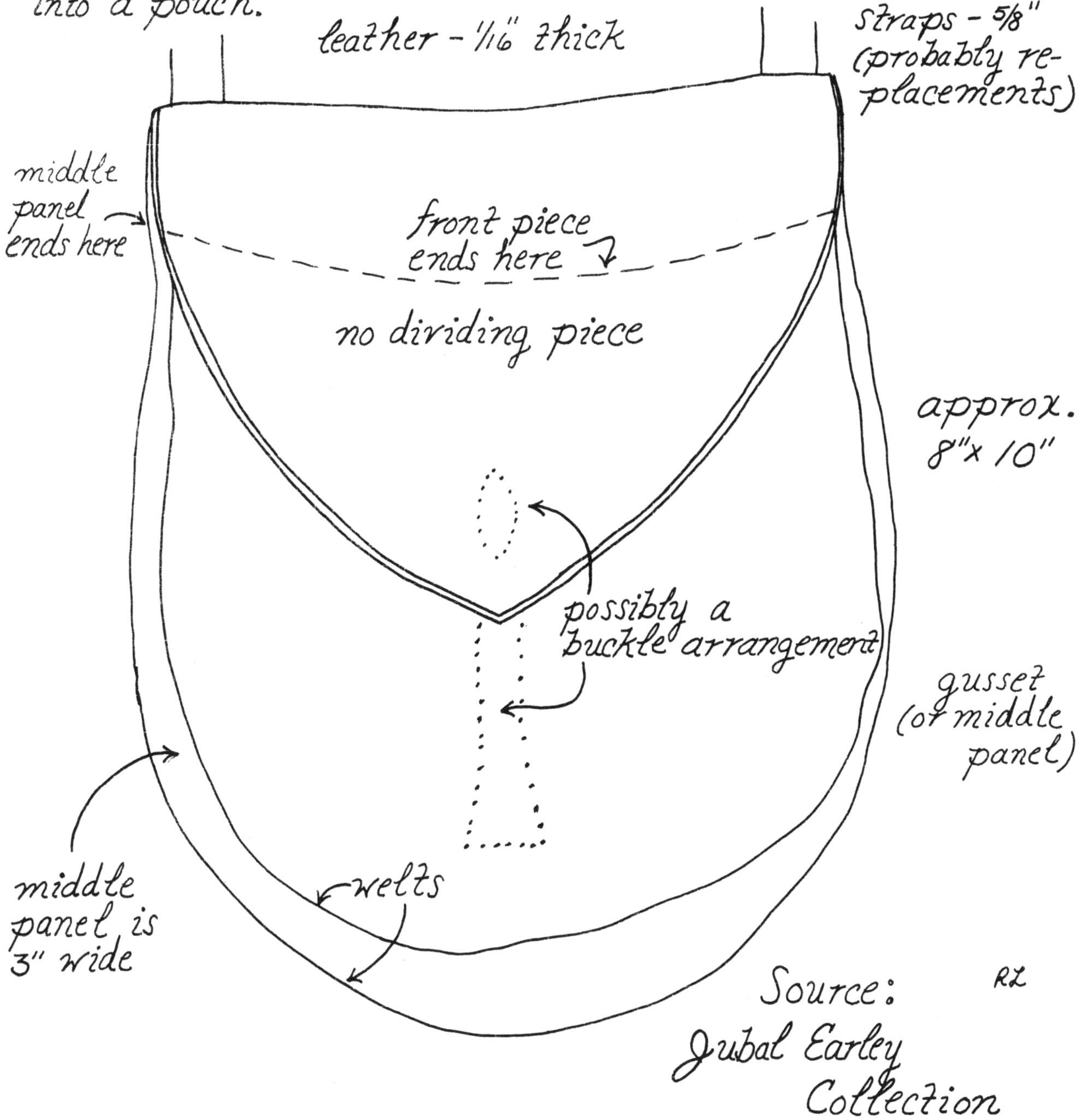

leather - 1/16" thick

straps - 5/8" (probably re-placements)

middle panel ends here

front piece ends here ↓

no dividing piece

approx. 8" x 10"

possibly a buckle arrangement

gusset (or middle panel)

middle panel is 3" wide

welts

Source: Jubal Earley Collection

RL

Hunting Pouches (cont'd.)

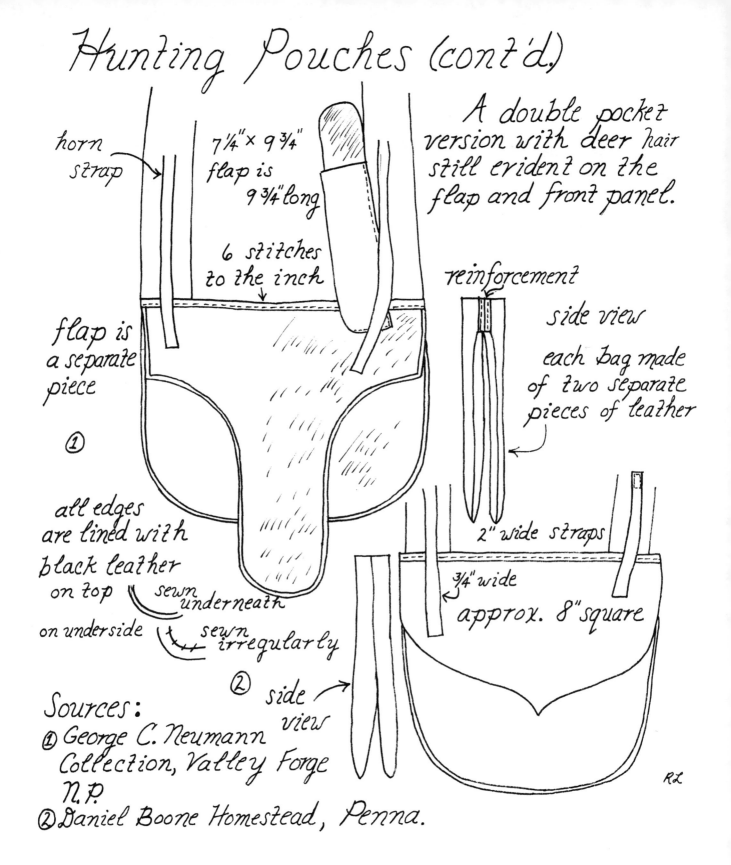

A double pocket version with deer hair still evident on the flap and front panel.

horn strap

7¼" × 9¾" flap is 9¾" long

6 stitches to the inch

flap is a separate piece

①

all edges are lined with black leather on top — sewn underneath

on underside — sewn irregularly

② side view

reinforcement

side view

each bag made of two separate pieces of leather

2" wide straps

¾" wide

approx. 8" square

Sources:
① George C. Neumann Collection, Valley Forge N.P.
② Daniel Boone Homestead, Penna.

RL

Hunting Pouch/Haversack

This rare, rather large artifact, was found with a flintlock smoothbore in south-central Pennsylvania. It is impossible to determine whether it was used as a hunting pouch or a haversack, possibly both. It was not used as a gamebag as no bloodstains could be found.

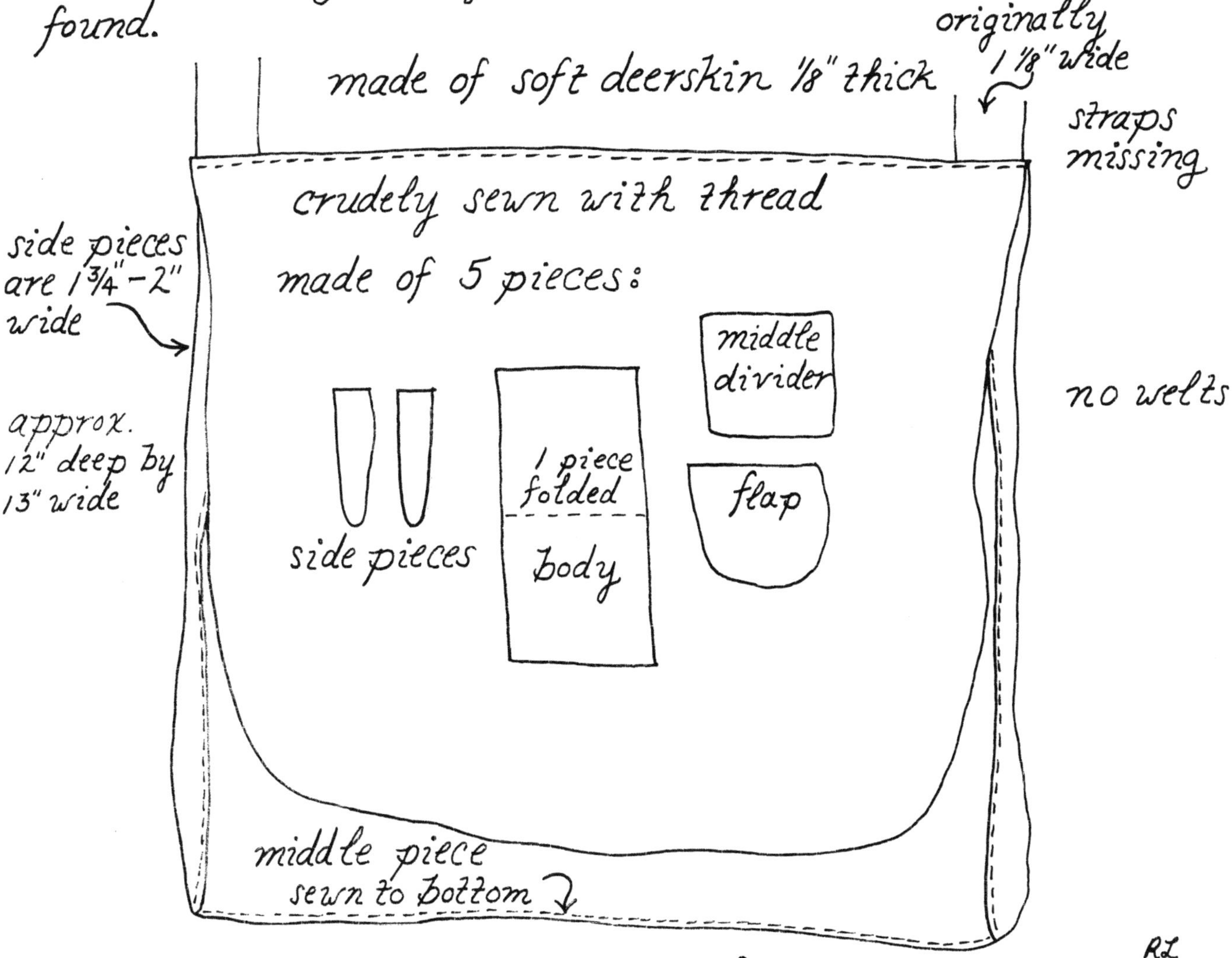

made of soft deerskin 1/8" thick

originally 1 1/8" wide

straps missing

crudely sewn with thread

made of 5 pieces:

side pieces are 1 3/4"–2" wide

approx. 12" deep by 13" wide

middle divider

side pieces

1 piece folded

body

flap

no welts

middle piece sewn to bottom

RL

Source:
Jubal Earley Collection

Knapsacks, Haversacks

In the eighteenth century there was a definite distinction between the knapsack and the haversack. The former was quite commonly used to carry equipment and personal belongings, and the latter used for rations. The state that the haversack would achieve after a few weeks of use probably would have curtailed it's being pressed into any other function.

Constructed of a heavy, coarse, grey linen, this knapsack is a typical speciman. The straps (missing) were probably made of leather and averaged about 1¾ inches for the shoulder straps, and ¾ to 1 inch wide for the fastenings on the bottom.

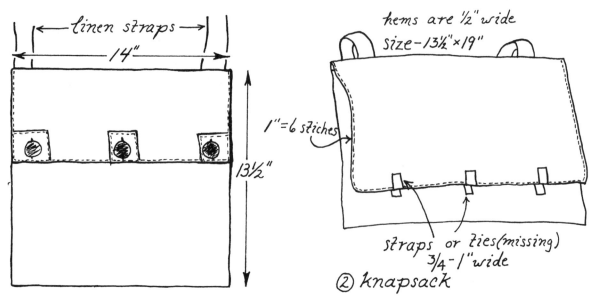

linen straps
14"
13½"
① haversack

hems are ½" wide
size—13½"×19"
1"=6 stiches
straps or ties(missing)
3/4 - 1"wide
② knapsack

Source: ① Wash. H.Q. Museum, Newburgh, N.Y. ② Fort Ticonderoga, N.Y.

Shot or Bullet Pouches

Shown here are several styles of the home-made bags or pouches used for holding lead balls or shot. No two were ever alike. The most common materials were tanned leather, rawhide, or cloth.

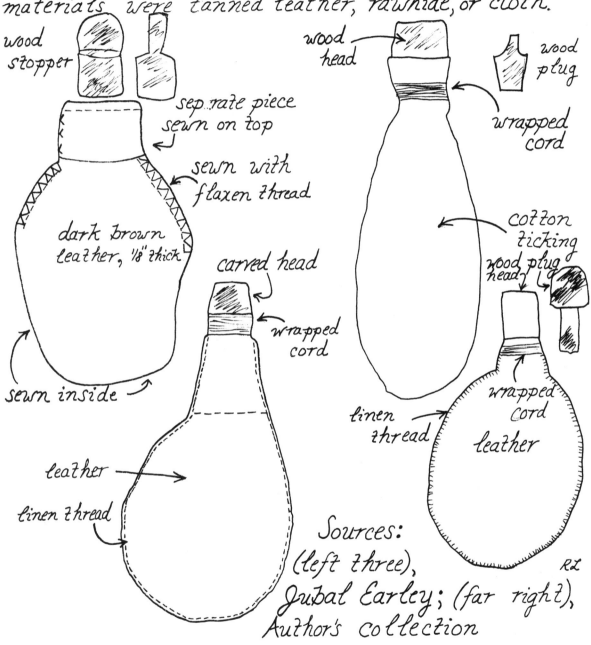

wood stopper

separate piece sewn on top

sewn with flaxen thread

dark brown leather, 1/8" thick

sewn inside

carved head

wrapped cord

leather

linen thread

wood head

wood plug

wrapped cord

cotton ticking

wood plug head

wrapped cord

linen thread

wrapped cord

leather

Sources: (left three), Jubal Earley; (far right), Author's collection

RL

Bullet Moulds

An indispensable item in every rifleman's hunting bag, bullet moulds were individually cut to fit each rifle's caliber. The early moulds were often a bit more bulky, and unlike the later examples, lacked a sprue cutter.

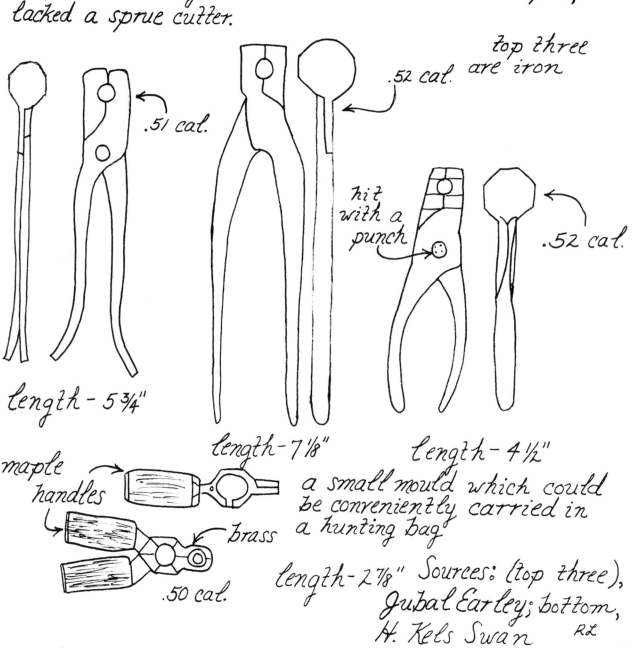

top three are iron

.52 cal.

.51 cal.

hit with a punch

.52 cal.

length - 5¾"

length - 7⅛"

length - 4½"
a small mould which could be conveniently carried in a hunting bag

maple handles

brass

.50 cal.

length - 2⅞" Sources: (top three), Jubal Earley; bottom, H. Kels Swan

RL

Canteen (pint-size)

Since riflemen were often sent out on short patrols to scout or reconnoiter, some were possibly issued pint-size canteens, rather than usual quart-sized versions, in order to reduce any unnecessary weight. The construction is very similar to that of a keg or barrel.

materials:

      staves - pine
      hoops - hickory
      heads - white oak

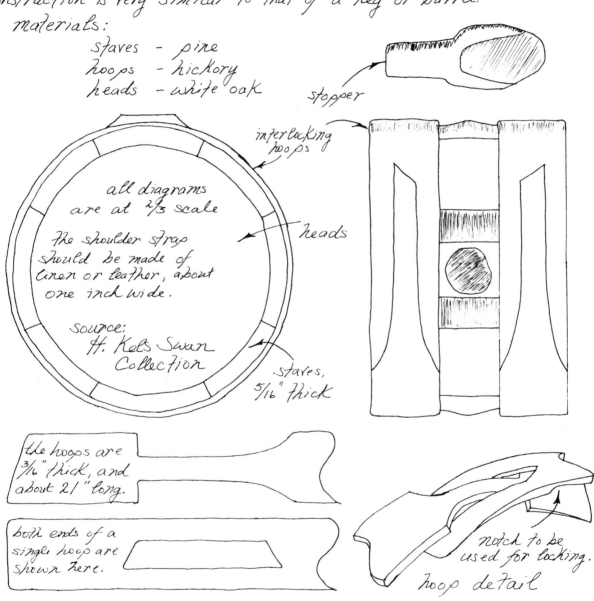

stopper

interlocking hoops

all diagrams are at 2/3 scale

the shoulder strap should be made of linen or leather, about one inch wide.

source:
H. Kels Swan Collection

heads

staves, 5/16" thick

the hoops are 3/16" thick, and about 21" long.

both ends of a single hoop are shown here.

notch to be used for locking.

hoop detail

Canteen   (rundlet)

A great variety of containers were pressed into service during the American Revolution to hold the soldiers water or rum ration, with wooden vessels being the most common. The little wooden "water bottle" pictured here was a favorite in the milita. It was carried on the left side, as were most canteens, by a leather strap or thong. The lathe cuts around the outside give the impression of reinforcing straps.

This particular example came from the Reading area of Buck's County, Pennsylvania, and was carried during the War for Independence by one "H. V. D.". It is dated 1776 and inscribed with the words "**Liberty X Death**". Due to the location where it was found, and it's pint-size capacity, it was probably carried by a rifleman.

shown at 1/2 scale

source:
H. Kels Swan Collection

holes for thong

lathe cuts

3/4 inch hole, stopper missing

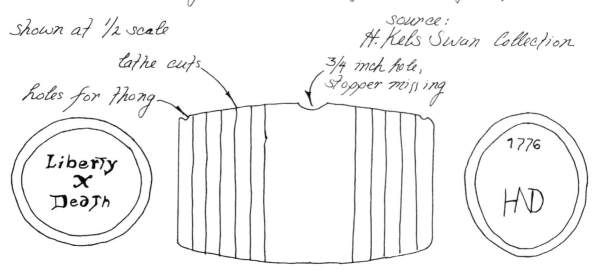

Liberty
X
Death

1776

HVD

Dog Tag with Wallet

This dog tag is the oldest known in America and was made and carried by Wilmer Cooper, a rifleman of Culpeper, Virginia. It is complete with its crude homemade wallet.

In 1777, Cooper was transferred to the "Commander-in-chiefs' Guard" at Morristown, New Jersey under the command of Captain Caleb Gibbs.

GIVE ME
LIBERTY OR
DEATH

15 VIRGINIA REG
PT. WILME COOPER

NOVEM. 1776

Approx. size
2½" × 4"

DON'T TRED

ON ME WC

Wallet:

made of two equal size pieces of leather (1/16" thick) and sewn with thick flaxen thread.

deerskin patch (glued) ———→

Made of
horn

open

WC

One of the members, James Jameson's company discovered the flag prior to the Co's. departure for Williamsburg:

"The flag had in the center a rattlesnake coiled in the act to strike, below were the words 'Don't tred on me!' At the sides, 'Liberty or Death!' and at the top, 'The Culpeper Minute Men!'."

Source:
H. Kels Swan Collection

167

Cups and Mugs

Tin cups were something of a luxury item for most frontier families. However, horn cups or mugs were quite common and were attractive and easy enough to make. Drinking vessels of copper were even traded to the Indians.

3¼"

holds one pint

5⁵⁄₁₆"

Tinned Sheet
¹⁄₆₄" thick.

There are very few 18th century tin cups in existence and illustrated here are two unearthed in Pennsylvania made of tinned sheet-iron and very well soldered together.

← 3½" →

To be attached to the belt sometimes a thong was tied to the handle but a more effective method was to tie a thong to a stick which could be shoved in and out of the belt without having to unbuckle it and remove it everytime.

Tied

thong

Stick

Frontiersman's horn cup, approximately 2½" at the base and 3" high. Base is made of a block of wood and attached with iron nails.

Frontiersman's horn cup

handle bent over →

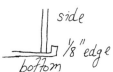

side
⅛" edge
bottom

edge of tin rolled over wire.

Cups and Mugs (con't.)

A horn mug or cup, dated 1779, found in the upper Hudson River Valley in New York State.

It has no handle and is typical of what a rifleman might make for himself. Sometimes they were artistically scrimshawed.

4.

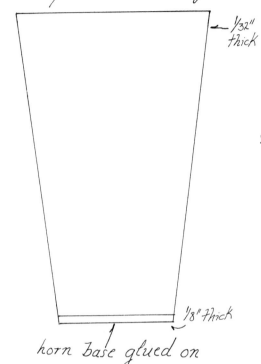

← 1/32" thick

1/8" Thick

horn base glued on

5.

A copper cup made of tinned sheet copper and traded to the Cherokees. Bottom is missing. No handle.

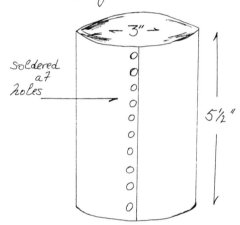

← 3" →

soldered at holes

5½"

Sources:
1 and 2 - Fort L.
3 - Point State Park (Ft. Pitt Museum) Pa., Historical and Museum Commission.
4 - Swan Collection of the Amer. Rev.
5 - Museum of the Cherokee Indian, North Carolina

Ladle & Melting Pot

iron, 1/10" thick

actual size   (12 5/8" long)

All frontier homesteads needed
these necessary implements just
as much as the bullet moulds which
accompanied them. The pot was used for melting
the bars of lead, and the ladle for scooping out the
hot liquid and pouring it into the mould.

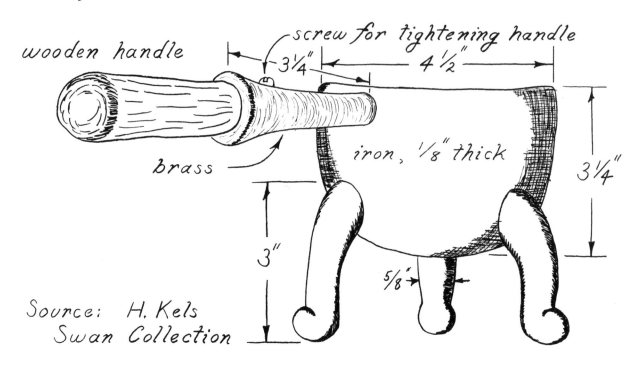

wooden handle

screw for tightening handle

3 1/4"   4 1/2"

brass

iron, 1/8" thick

3 1/4"

3"

5/8"

Source: H. Kels
Swan Collection

Miscellaneous

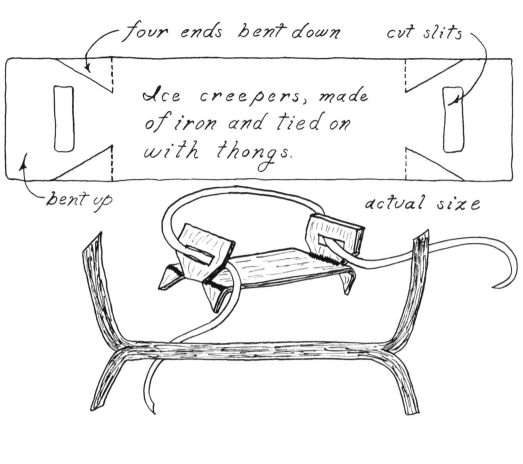

four ends bent down   cut slits

Ice creepers, made
of iron and tied on
with thongs.

bent up   actual size

Flint and tinder
box constructed of
wrought iron, and
complete with flint,
striker, and tow
linen tinder

shown actual size

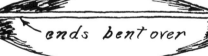

ends bent over

side view of box and striker

Miscellaneous (cont'd.)

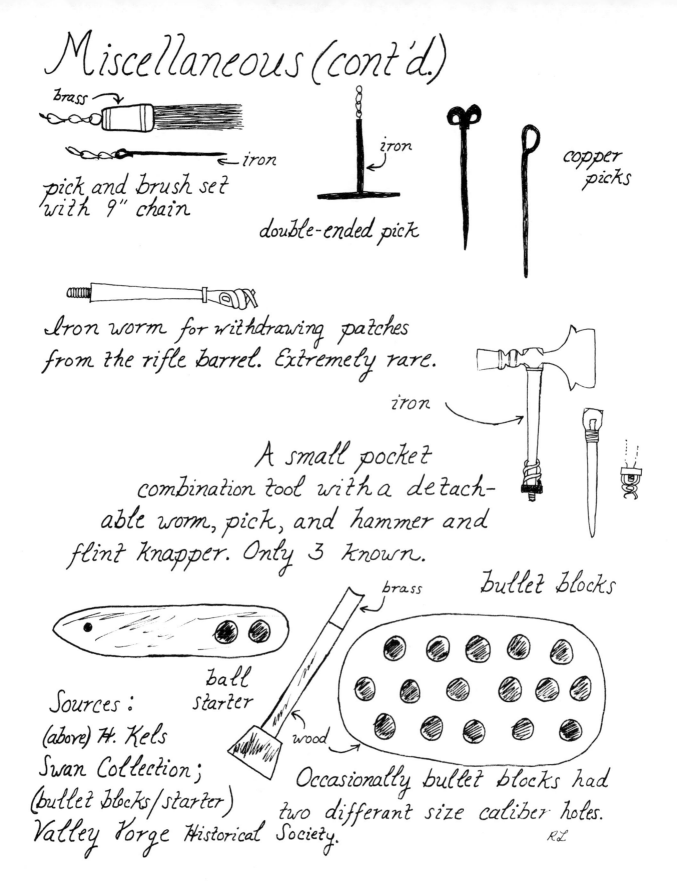

brass

←— iron

pick and brush set
with 9" chain

iron

double-ended pick

copper
picks

Iron worm for withdrawing patches
from the rifle barrel. Extremely rare.

iron

A small pocket
combination tool with a detach-
able worm, pick, and hammer and
flint knapper. Only 3 known.

bullet blocks

brass

ball
starter

wood

Sources:
(above) H. Kels
Swan Collection;
(bullet blocks/starter)
Valley Forge Historical Society.

Occasionally bullet blocks had
two different size caliber holes.

RL

172

Miscellaneous (cont'd.)

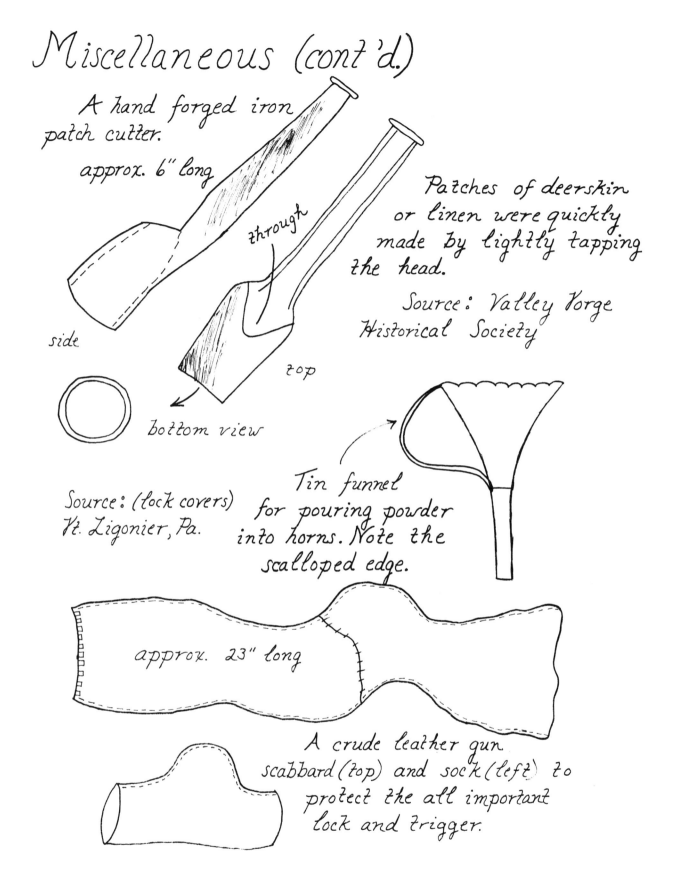

A hand forged iron patch cutter.

approx. 6" long

Patches of deerskin or linen were quickly made by lightly tapping the head.

Source: Valley Forge Historical Society

side

through

top

bottom view

Source: (lock covers) Ft. Ligonier, Pa.

Tin funnel for pouring powder into horns. Note the scalloped edge.

approx. 23" long

A crude leather gun scabbard (top) and sock (left) to protect the all important lock and trigger.

BIBLIOGRAPHY

BIBLIOGRAPHY

PRIMARY SOURCES:

Anburey, Thomas, *Travels Through the Interior Parts of America*, 2 vols., London, 1791.

Boyd, Julian P., ed., *The Papers of Thomas Jefferson*, 9 vols., Princeton, NJ, 1950, 1954.

Burgoyne, John, *A Study of the Expedition From Canada, as Laid Before The House of Commons*, London, 1780.

Chastellux, Francois Jean, Marquis de, *Travels in North America, in the Years 1780, 1781, and 1782*, New York, 1827.

Clark, George Rogers, *George Rogers Clark Papers, 1771-1781, 1781-1784*, vols. 8 and 19, Illinois State Historical Collections, Springfield, IL, 1912, 1924.
  Colonel George Rogers Clark's Sketch of His Campaign in The Illinois in 1778-79, Columbus, O, 1869.

Clinton, George, *Public Papers of George Clinton, First Governor of New York*, 10 vols., ed. by Hugh Hastings, Albany, 1899-1914.

Collins, James, *A Revolutionary Soldier*, Clinton, LA, 1859. Reprinted, New York, 1979.

Cresswell, Nicholas, *Journal of Nicholas Cresswell, 1774-1777*, New York, 1924.

Doddridge, Rev. Joseph, *Notes on the Settlements and Indian Wars of the Western Parts of Virginia and Pennsylvania, 1763-1783*, Albany, 1876.

Fitzpatrick, John C., *The Writings of Washington*, 38 vols., Washington, DC, 1931-1944.

Hanger, George, *Notes to All Sportsmen*, London, 1814.

Henry, John Joseph, *Account of Arnold's Campaign Against Quebec and of the Hardships and Sufferings of that Band of Heroes Who Traversed the Wilderness of Maine from Cambridge to the St. Lawrence, in the Autumn of 1775*, Lancaster, PA, 1812. Reprinted Albany, NY, 1877.

Lamb, Roger, *An Original and Authentic Journal of Occurances During the Late American War*, 1809. Reprinted New York, Arno Press, 1968.

Smith, James, *An Account of the Remarkable Occurances in the Life and Travels of Colonel James Smith, During His Captivity with the Indians, in the Years 1755, 1756, 1757, 1758 and 1759*, Lexington, KY, 1799. Reprinted Robert Clark & Co., Cincinnati, OH, 1870.

Smythe, J.F.D., *Tour in the United States of America*, Chapter 23, 1784, pp. 178-183.

Thatcher, Dr. James, *Military Journal During the American Revolution from 1775 to 1783*, Boston, 1823.

Timberlake, Lt. Henry, *Lieutenant Henry Timberlake's Memoirs, 1756-1763*, Samuel Cole Williams, ed., Johnson City, TN, 1927.

Weld, Isaac, *Travels Through the States of North America, 1795-1797*, London, 1807.

SECONDARY SOURCES:

Arnow, Harriet Simpson, *Seedtime On The Cumberland*, New York, 1960.
  Flowering Of The Cumberland, New York, 1963.

Boatner, Mark M., III, *Encyclopedia of the American Revolution*, New York, 1966.

Bolton, Charles K., *The Private Soldier Under Washington*, New York, 1902.

Callahan, North, *Daniel Morgan, Ranger of the Revolution*, New York, 1961.

Copeland, Peter, *Working Dress in Colonial and Revolutionary America*, Westport, CT, 1977.

Cruickshank, Ernest A., *The Story of Butler's Rangers and the Settlement of Niagara*, Welland, Ont., Canada, 1893.

Dandridge, Danske, *American Prisoners of the Revolution*, Charlottesville, VA, 1911. Reprinted Baltimore, Geneological Publishing Co., 1967.

Dillin, John, *The Kentucky Rifle*, Washington, DC, 1924.

Forroy, Richard Reuben, *Edward Hand; His Role in the American Revolution*, Ph.D. dissertation, Drake University, Des Moines, IA, 1976.

Graham, James, *The Life of General Daniel Morgan*, New York, 1859.

Graymont, Barbara, *The Iroquois in the American Revolution*, Syracuse, 1972.

Grimm, Jacob L., *Archaeological Investigations of Fort Ligonier, 1960-1965*, Pittsburgh, 1970.

Hagan, Edward, *War In Schohary*, Middleburgh, NY, 1980.

Higginbotham, Don, *Daniel Morgan, Revolutionary Rifleman*, Chapel Hill, NC, 1961.

Kaufman, Henry J., *The Pennsylvania-Kentucky Rifle*, Harrisburg, PA, 1960.

Ketchum, Richard, M., *American Heritage History of the Revolution*, New York, 1958.

Millis, Walter, *Arms and Men*, New York, 1956.

Montross, Lynn, *Rag, Tag and Bobtail, The Story of the Continental Army, 1775-1783*, New York, 1952.

Moore, Warren, *Weapons of the American Revolution*, New York, 1967.

Neumann, George C., *The History of Weapons of the American Revolution*, New York, 1972.

Peterson, Harold L., *Arms and Armor in Colonial America 1526-1783*, Harrisburg, PA, 1956.
   The Book of the Continental Soldier, Harrisburg, PA, 1968.

Roosevelt, Theodore, *The Winning of the West*, 4 vols., New York, 1917.

Selby, John, *The Road to Yorktown*, New York, 1976.

Sosin, Jack M., *The Revolutionary Frontier, 1763-1783*, New York, 1976.

Swiggett, Howard, *War Out Of Niagara: Walter Butler and the Tory Rangers*, New York, 1933.

Trevelyan, Sir George Otto, *The American Revolution*, 6 vols., New York, 1909.

Van Every, Dale, *A Company of Heroes: The American Frontier, 1775-1783*, New York, 1962.

Ward, Christopher, *War of the Revolution*, 2 vols., New York, 1952.

Williams, Samuel Cole, *Tennessee During the Revolutionary War*, Nashville, 1944.

Wright, Colonel John Womack, *Some Notes on the Continental Army*, Cornwallville, NY, 1975.

CONTEMPORARY PERIODICALS:

London Chronicle, 1775.

Maryland Gazette, 1756.

Pennsylvania Gazette, 1775.

Pennsylvania Packet, 1775.

Virginia Gazette, 1775-1776.

American Observer, 1775.

INDEX

INDEX

Richard B. LaCrosse, Jr. is a graduate of the State University College at Brockport, New York with a B.S. degree in History. He has been employed by the National Park Service at Fort Stanwix National Monument in Rome, New York, Morristown National Historical Park in Morristown, New Jersey, 18th Century Restorations (a company specializing in the preservation of antique buildings), and is currently with the Ontario State Historical Site, New York.

Mr. LaCrosse is currently a member of several historical organizations including the Brigade of the American Revolution - an association dedicated to accurately portraying the common soldier during the War for Independence. *The Frontier Rifleman* is Mr. LaCrosse's first book. He has had several magazine articles published by local historical societies as well as the *Dixie Gun Works Black Powder Annual*. In addition he has appeared as an "extra" in the movies *Sweet Liberty* and *Alamo, the Price of Freedom*.

Mr. LaCrosse lives with his wife, Leslie, in a restored 18th century log home in Parish, New York.